16

THE OLD SCHOOL

THE OLD SCHOOL

Essays by Divers Hands

EDITED BY
GRAHAM GREENE

Oxford
OXFORD UNIVERSITY PRESS
1984

Oxford University Press, Walton Street, Oxford OX2 6DP

London New York Toronto
Delhi Bombay Calcutta Madras Karachi
Kuala Lumpur Singapore Hong Kong Tokyo
Nairobi Dar es Salaam Cape Town
Melbourne Auckland

and associated companies in
Beirut Berlin Ibadan Mexico City Nicosia

Oxford is a trade mark of Oxford University Press

First published 1934 by Jonathan Cape Ltd.
This edition first issued as an Oxford University Press paperback 1984

British Library Cataloguing in Publication Data
The Old school.—(Oxford paperbacks)
1. Students—Great Britain   2. Schools—Great Britain
I. Greene, Graham
371.8'092'2   LA631.8
ISBN 0-19-281484-2

Printed in Great Britain by
Richard Clay (The Chaucer Press) Ltd.
Bungay, Suffolk

CONTENTS

CONTENTS

Grammar School by H. E. Bates reprinted by permission of Laurence Pollinger Ltd

Hot-Water-Bottle Love by Theodora Benson reprinted by permission of the Literary Executor of Theodora Benson

The Mulberry Tree by Elizabeth Bowen reprinted by permission of Curtis Brown Ltd., Literary Executors of the Estate of Elizabeth Bowen

The Conformer by L. P. Hartley reprinted by permission of Miss A. N. Hartley

Pity the Pedagogue by Harold Nicolson reprinted by permission of Nigel Nicolson

An Irish Schooling reprinted by permission of Seán O'Faoláin

The Gothic Arch by William Plomer reprinted by permission of Sir Rupert Hart-Davis

The Wat'ry Glade by Anthony Powell reprinted by permission of David Higham Associates

Day Boy by Stephen Spender reprinted by permission of A. D. Peters & Co. Ltd.

Pioneers by E. L. Grant Watson reprinted by permission of David Higham Associates

A Child of the Five Wounds by Antonia White is reproduced with the permission of the Literary Executrices of Antonia White

The Last Word by Graham Green reprinted by permission of Laurence Pollinger Ltd.

While every effort has been made to secure permission, we may have failed in a few cases to trace the copyright holder. We apologize for any apparent negligence.

PREFACE

I REGARD this book rather as a premature memorial, like a family photograph album, a gathering of the staid and unloved hovering, in the most absurd headgear, unconsciously 'upon the brink' and occasionally among them, in a deerstalker cap or a hobble skirt, somebody who has betrayed one's natural distrust of human nature, somebody one has loved and will miss. Like the family album, this book will, I hope, be superficially more funny than tragic, for so odd a system of education does not demand a pompous memorial.

For there can be small doubt that the system which this book mainly represents is doomed. Too few people to-day can afford the fees of a public school. The state-aided pupils are within the gates, but the geese doze under their B.A. hoods around the Capitol. For how class-conscious these schools remain. I remember how at my own solidly middle class school we despised the boys from the elementary schools. They were popularly supposed not to wash and to tell lies more readily than the rest of us and we laughed at their accents. But I do not think we were to blame; we were not naturally class-conscious; it was from the masters we learnt our snobbery and the means to express it.

Whatever the political changes in this country during the next few years one thing surely is almost certain: the class distinctions will not remain unaltered and the public school, as it exists to-day, will disappear. Where then but in this book will the social historian discover a true picture of the vanished system? Not in the generalizations of progressive critics, any more than in the sentimental memories of speech-day orators, for their experience is necessarily limited. Here he will find examples not only of the public school, but of the elementary school, the grammar school, the convent school, the co-educational school. He will find a little that is good and a little that is astonishingly bad and a great deal that is almost too funny to be true.

But it must be clearly understood that the truth is of a particular period. Most of the writers were at school in the years of the war or the years immediately after the war. It is quite open to any school to deny that the description still applies. The ideal critics of this book would be found among the boys now at school.

HONOUR

[Gresham's School, Holt]

BY W. H. AUDEN

No account of school life ever appears disinterested to those who disagree with it: it will always appear the work of either a nest-fouler or a nest whitewasher. I can only say that if, in my account of Gresham's School, Holt, I am sometimes critical, it is not, I hope, from personal motives. Of its fairness and accuracy I must leave those directly acquainted with the school in the first half of the last decade to judge.

As what one sees depends on what one is, I must begin with a description of myself at that time. The son of book-loving, Anglo-Catholic parents of the professional class, the youngest of three brothers, I was — and in most respects still am — mentally precocious, physically backward, short-sighted, a rabbit at all games, very untidy and grubby, a nail-biter, a physical coward, dishonest, sentimental, with no community sense whatever, in fact a typical little highbrow and difficult child. It says much — or perhaps little — for Holt that I was never bullied or molested, I was allowed to make my friends where I chose, and was, taking everything into consideration, very happy throughout my time there.

The first condition for a successful school is a beautiful situation and in that respect we were at Holt very fortunate. The school authorities, with extraordinary good sense, set virtually no bounds, a liberty rarely I believe abused. Watching a snow storm come up from the sea over the marshes at Salthouse, and walking in a June dawn (not so legally) by Hempstead Mill are only the two most vivid of a hundred such experiences.

If the buildings were not lovely — their date precluded that — they were better than many, and comfortable. Class-rooms were warm and well-lit. In my own house we had dormitories with cubicles (smaller dormitories of 4 or 6 beds without cubicles would be better I think) and studies, shared with two or three others for the first two years, and single afterwards: so we cannot be said to have been unduly herded together. Fagging, during one's first year or so, was extremely light, hot water was plentiful, and the cooking, if undistinguished — no one seems ever to have solved the problem of school maids who are almost invariably slatternly and inefficient — was quite adequate.

So much for the surroundings which were all that a parent could desire. What about the education?

On the academic side I can't say much because I remember so little, but I imagine it was pretty good. Holt is a modern school, i.e. it does not teach Greek and concentrate on science, history, etc. We had a magnificent library, perhaps the only requisite because real people, who can learn, given that chance, will teach themselves; the labs were excellently equipped, all the staff were conscientious and some efficient, and our scholarship list was quite satisfactory.

As regards out-of-school activities the school was extremely sensible. Athletics were treated as they ought to be treated, as something to be enjoyed and not made a fetish of, every kind of hobby was encouraged (I remember with special pleasure the expeditions of the sociological society which did no more sociology than my foot, but had a grand time visiting factories in a charabanc). There was plenty of acting, house plays in the winter and a Shakespeare play in an open-air theatre in the summer. And if I think that all out-of-door plays are detestable, that is a personal prejudice.

I can't say that we were given any real sense of the problems of the world, or of how to attack them, other than in vague ideals of service, but then I have never heard of any school that did, and my own convictions are perhaps too extreme for me to expect to see them acted upon. Indeed it is impossible to see how any school, which is not directly attached in some way to an industrial or agricultural unit, and where boys and staff are both drawn from the monied classes, can hope to see the world picture of that class objectively. The mass production of gentlemen is their *raison-d'être*, and one can hardly suggest that they should adopt principles which would destroy them. The fact remains that the public school boy's attitude to the working-class and to the not-quite-quite has altered very little since the war. He is taught to be fairly kind and polite, provided of course they return the compliment, but their lives and needs remain as remote to him as those of another species. And I doubt very much if the same isn't true of the staff as well. I do remember hearing however that a master was sacked for taking part in left-wing politics outside the school, which if true, and I cannot vouch for the accuracy of the story, seems to me a shameful thing.

The only concrete suggestion I have to make here is that the staff might give up wearing those ridiculous black clothes (if they still do) which made them look like unsuccessful insurance agents, and certainly did not increase our respect for them; if we were allowed – and rightly – to wear blazers and flannel trousers, the staff as well might surely be allowed a sensible costume.

I suppose no one ever remembers actually being taught anything, though one remembers clearly enough when one failed to learn. My efforts at engineering which must have been as distressing to the very nice military man who taught that subject as they were boring to me — the sum total of my achievement was two battered ash-trays and any number of ruined tools — are still vivid.

Where one was more successful, one remembers only the idiosyncrasies of the masters, that X shouted in class — a horrible habit — that Y would come up behind one on a bicycle ride and pinch one's seat, that Z wore his cap like a racing-tout, and so on. For, as people, those who at one time or another have taught me stand out in my memory very clearly, far more clearly in fact than my friends, and this seems a common experience.

It is perhaps as well that teachers can never realize

how intensely aware of their personalities their charges are, because if they could they would be too terrified to move or to open their mouths. A single act or remark is quite sufficient to queer the pitch. For example a certain master once caught me writing poetry in prep, writing a poem which I knew to be a bad one. He said 'You shouldn't waste your sweetness on the desert air like this, Auden'; to-day I cannot think of him without wishing him evil.

It is pleasant to turn from such thoughts to remember two men to whom I owe an immense debt, the master who taught Classics and English, and the Music master. The former, who was never tired of showing us the shallowness of those who despised the classics, had the most magnificent bass reading voice I have ever heard, and from listening to him read the Bible or Shakespeare I learnt more about poetry and the humanities than from any course of University lectures.

To the latter I owe not only such knowledge of music as I possess, but my first friendship with a grown up person, with all that that means. As a musician he was in the first rank. I do not think it was only partiality that made me feel, when later I heard Schweitzer play Bach on the organ, that he played no better.

As a person he was what the ideal schoolmaster should be, ready to be a friend and not a beak, to give the adolescent all the comfort and stimulus of a personal relation, without at the same time making any demands for himself in return, a temptation which

5

must assail all those who are capable of attracting and influencing their juniors. He was in the best sense of the word indifferent, and if the whole of the rest of my schooldays had been hateful, which they weren't, his existence alone would make me recall them with pleasure.

Finally, no acknowledgments of mine would be complete without a reference to one — call him Wreath — who though not a member of the staff, yet as captain of my house when I was still a junior, stood to me in much the same relation. A really good prefect is as rare as a comet — authority makes most boys of eighteen or any other age into stuck-up little idiots, but he was a born leader and the only person, boy or master, who ever made the conventional house and school loyalties have any meaning for me.

I have no wish to belittle a profession to which I have the honour to belong. Its members are practically all extremely conscientious, hard working, keen on their job, and sometimes very intelligent. At the same time if one were invited to dine with a company representing all trades and professions, the schoolmaster is the last person one would want to sit next to. Being a schoolmaster is not like being a Bank Clerk — it is not enough just to be efficient at teaching; one must be a remarkable person. Some schoolmasters are, but far, far too many are silted-up old maids, earnest young scoutmasters, or just generally dim.

Some of the reasons for this are clear; in the first place the profession has generally to be entered young, and those of university age who are attracted

to it are rarely the most vital and adventurous spirits.
On the contrary they are only too often those who are
afraid of the mature world, either the athletic whose
schooldays were the peak of their triumph from which
they dread to recede, or else the timid academic whose
qualifications or personal charm are insufficient to
secure them a fellowship; in either case the would-be
children. It is not improbable that those who enter
teaching as a *pis-aller*, as they might become steve-
dores or bootleggers, are often the best; which may be
the reason why the staffs of preparatory schools seem
so superior to those of public schools.

In the second place, partly because they have never
had the chance, and sometimes I am ashamed to say
as the result of a definite policy of the school authorities, they have no outside interests. This seems to me
disastrous, leading inevitably to them becoming either
lifeless prunes or else spiritual vampires, sucking
their vitality from these children. Indeed if I were a
headmaster — which heaven forbid — I would have
no unmarried man on my staff who was not definitely
engaged on some work outside the school. Better
still, the number of professional teachers would be very
small, the product of a very vigorous selection. The
rest would be conscripted, every citizen after some
years in the world would be called up to serve his
two or three years teaching for the state, after which he
would return to his job again. However that is only a
daydream and I must return to Holt and its education
of our morals.

That side was run on what was called the honour

system, and for the benefit of those who do not know the school, some explanation of this is necessary.

About a week after arrival every new boy was interviewed separately by his housemaster and the headmaster — half watt hypnotism we used to call it — and was asked — I need hardly say how difficult it would have been to refuse — to promise on his honour three things.

(1) Not to swear.

(2) Not to smoke.

(3) Not to say or do anything indecent.

Having done so, two consequences followed:

(1) If you broke any of these promises you should report the breakage to your housemaster.

(2) If you saw anyone else break them, you should endeavour to persuade him to report and if he refused you should report him yourself.

Before I say anything in criticism, I must add that the system worked, in public at any rate. One almost never saw anyone smoking, heard anyone swear, or came across any smut. From the point of view of master and parent it would seem ideal. Here at last was the clean and healthy school they had been looking for.

From the boy's point of view on the other hand, I feel compelled to say that I believe no more potent engine for turning them into neurotic innocents, for perpetuating those very faults of character which it was intended to cure, was ever devised.

Everyone knows that the only emotion that is fully developed in a boy of fourteen is the emotion of loyalty and honour. For that very reason it is so dangerous. By appealing to it, you can do almost anything you choose, you can suppress the expression of all those emotions, particularly the sexual, which are still undeveloped; like a modern dictator you can defeat almost any opposition from other parts of the psyche, but if you do, if you deny these other emotions their expression and development, however silly or shocking they may seem to you, they will not only never grow up, but they will go backward, for human nature cannot stay still; they will, like all things that are shut up, go bad on you.

Of the two consequences of our promises, the second, the obligation to interfere with one's neighbour, is of course much the more serious. It meant that the whole of our moral life was based on fear, on fear of the community, not to mention the temptation it offered to the natural informer, and fear is not a healthy basis. It makes one furtive and dishonest and unadventurous. The best reason I have for opposing Fascism is that at school I lived in a Fascist state. Of the effect of the system on the boys after they left school I have little direct experience outside my own and those whom I knew personally, but all those with whom I have spoken, whether old boys or others who have come into contact with old boys, have borne out my conclusion that the effect is a serious one in many cases. I am fully aware that the first five years of life are more important than any others and that those cases I am thinking of would have had a difficult time anyway, but I am convinced that their difficulties were enormously and unnecessarily increased by the honour system. Though the system was a peculiarity of Holt, it is only an extreme example of a tendency which can be seen in the running of every school; the tendency to identify the welfare of the school with the welfare of the boys in it, to judge school life not by its own peculiar standards as a stage in the development towards maturity, but as an end in itself by adult standards. Every headmaster is inclined to think that so long as all's fair in his own little garden he has succeeded. When later he sees what some of his old boys have turned into he seldom realizes that the very apparent perfection he was so proud of is partly responsible.

You can, I repeat, do almost anything by utilizing the sense of community so long as the community is there, but as soon as the pressure is removed your unfortunate pupils are left defenceless. Either the print has taken so deeply that they remain frozen and undeveloped, or else, their infantilized instinct suddenly released, they plunge into foolish and damaging dissipation.

The first truth a schoolmaster has to learn is that if the fool would persist in his folly he would become wise; in other words, to leave well alone and not to give advice until it is asked for, remembering that nearly all his education is done by the boy himself with the help of other boys of his own age. There is far too much talk about ideals at all schools. Ideals are the conclusions drawn from a man of experience, not the data: they are essentially for the mature.

Whether for good or ill dogmatic religion, that is to say a Christian world-picture, has broken down among schoolmasters, and religion without dogma soon becomes, as it was at Holt, nothing but vague uplift, as flat as an old bottle of soda water. For the young without experience ideals are as grave a danger in the moral sphere as book learning is in the intellectual, the danger of becoming a purely mental concept, mechanizing the soul.

In the absence of an orthodoxy, and we shall have to reconcile ourselves to that for some time, education has to rely almost entirely upon the quality of the teacher. For a teacher to be of real value to his pupils, he must be a mature and above all a happy person, giving the young the feeling that adult life is infinitely more exciting and interesting than their own, he must be prepared to give them all his powers of affection and imaginative understanding when they want them, yet to forget them completely the moment they are gone, to be indifferent to them personally; and lastly he must have no moral bees-in-his-bonnet, no preconceptions of what the good child should be; he must be shocked or alarmed at nothing, only patient to understand the significance of any piece of behaviour from the child's point of view, not his own; to see in the perfect little ape his most promising charge, and watchful to remove as tactfully and unobtrusively as possible such obstacles to progress as he can. He must, to use a phrase of Mr. Gerald Heard's, and I know no better, 'be an anthropologist'.

More nonsense is talked about education than

about anything else, and I cannot hope to do better than my fellow amateurs. I have written about Holt because I was there and therefore have known it from the inside, but any other school would have done as well. If I have criticized certain things, it is not because I think Holt is worse than other schools — in many respects it is probably considerably in advance of them — but because at a time like the present when the world into which our young emerge is bound to be a very difficult one, it is particularly important that they should get the best start we can give them, and too many suggestions are better than none. I offer mine for what they are worth.

GRAMMAR SCHOOL

[Kettering]

BY H. E. BATES

In a recent and well-known novel the principal male character — hardly a hero — is in the early part of the book a master at a newly-built grammar-school in the Midlands; the author has sketched-in the school, the common-room and the raw provincial town deftly and realistically — so well, in fact, that when I read the book I had no difficulty in recognizing the school as my own, the town as the one to which I had travelled by the early morning train for five years and the common-room as the one to which I had so often gone with a miserable sense of sickness and doom.

Looking back I find it hard to disentangle and arrange in comprehensible order the whole impressions of those years. But I remember the beginning, the first day, well enough. I am not quite sure, but I dare say my mother had bought me a new suit, ready-made, and that I had been made to clean my boots the night before, and to see that my season-ticket was safe in my waistcoat pocket. My parents were decidedly not well off and they were no doubt very pleased and proud when I won a scholarship entitling me to the benefits of higher education. I dare say they may have had vague and happy dreams of my becoming a cashier in a bank or a traveller in leather or perhaps even a school teacher, and I did not tell them that I had already decided to become a farmer, or failing that, a professional footballer. Even if I had told them I dare say they would not have minded. They were very proud of me. My grandfather was even prouder. It was he who was a farmer. 'The boy's a masterpiece!' he would say, taking off my cap. 'Look at his head! There's a head for you! There's something else in that head besides ticks.' No wonder that I too wanted to become a farmer. With a head like that it was hard for me to believe that I could benefit much from a higher education.

In truth I was very sick and very nervous when the first day arrived. I had been very happy at an elementary school, where life was crude and exciting and where there was no homework and no punishment except the cane. The school was in the heart of the roughest quarter of a raw industrial town. Almost every day there would be ructions, and those ructions had rules as strict as the laws governing a Greek tragedy. They would begin with the schoolmaster questioning a boy and this would be followed by the boy cheeking the schoolmaster and this by the boy being called to the front of the class. The second act began with the boy refusing to obey and this would be followed by the schoolmaster seizing the boy by the scruff of his neck and dragging him out and producing the cane. After that the boy would be ordered to hold out his hand. He would hold it out, the schoolmaster would raise his cane, the cane would descend, the boy whipping his hand safely behind his back as the stroke fell. At that point the schoolmaster would lose his temper. Up would go the cane and come down again in a mad smash on the boy's shoulders. The boy, whimpering with rage, would kick the master's shins until the bone rang hollow. This sublime and sensational drama would go on until, as though warned by some telegraphic magic, the boy's mother would appear, rolling up her blouse-sleeves, to avenge her offspring. The fury of the tiger defending its young is a mild emotion beside the fury with which a shoemaker's wife of 1910 would defend her son. And I have never been able to swallow, since that time, the notion that women were altogether the passive and gentler half of humanity.

Life at the elementary school had therefore been very vigorous and sensational. It would, I knew, be very different at the grammar-school. I had not read the school-stories of popular writers for nothing. I knew very well that the masters would wear black gowns and possibly mortar-boards too. The prefects would have studies in which they fried sausages and drank beer on the quiet in the middle of the night and those boys whose parents were a little better off would wear Eton collars and the little black jackets my grandfather called bum-starvers. I should have to learn Latin and French and a new kind of English in which words like cads and rotters, and expressions like bally bounders and beastly fellows, played a large part. Life was going to be on a higher plane altogether. I was prepared for that. What worried me was that a preparatory course in a crude industrial elementary school was hardly the best sort of training for this new educational flight. I was very nervous and my stomach kept turning watery and sick. If I had any consolation at all it was the memory of my grandfather's words.

The first day was a great shock. In the train a sinister gentleman with a club-foot and very black eyebrows and a dark smear of moustache asked me my name, my mother's name, my father's name, what my father did, whether I smoked, ordered me to call him sir, and then proceeded to knock me flat on my back in the carriage seat, leap on top of me and chastise my behind with a ruler. When he had finished I stood up and he knocked me down again. It was rather like the fight with the pale young gentleman in *Great Expectations*. When I recovered I was dusty and dishevelled and the sandwiches my mother had packed up for my dinner were squashed. Even so I was the neatest and best dressed boy in the carriage — so much so that I felt conspicuous. As though thinking this too another boy proceeded to knock me down, and a great many feet trampled on me and my behind was belted with a leather strap from the carriage window.

It was a severe, but not an extreme shock. I clung to my illusions. Life was going to be higher and different — there was no possible doubt of that. Horseplay and belting new boys' behinds was all very well out of school, but I knew that life in the school itself was going to be extremely serious and high-minded. I believe I hoped it was going to be aristocratic too.

At school, therefore, the shock was even greater. The school was newly built, of fresh red brick, not at all beautiful, and stood in a large asphalt playground. It was a little grander, but not much, than the school I had left. There were no quadrangles and no vast playing-fields of lovely grass with avenues of quiet elms. Inside there was a prevailing odour of floor-polish. The class-rooms seemed very like the class-rooms I had always known. The masters certainly wore black gowns but none of them had mortar-boards and none of the boys wore bum-starvers. I noticed that there were very few masters. It was the year 1916, a few months later than the opening chapters of the novel I have mentioned, and the masters who had become soldiers had been replaced by what I can only describe as females. These creatures were divided into two classes: the repressed and terrified, and the masculine and horsy. The subject they taught automatically became the subjects I hated. Looking back now, I know that, under other conditions, they would have been the subjects I should naturally have loved.

I was of course a clever boy. Hadn't I won a scholar-ship and hadn't my grandfather pointed out the extraordinary size of my head? Hadn't I diddled the elementary school-teachers with catchy questions about the magnetic pole and the lost tribes of Israel? There was no doubt that in due course I should become something very much out of the ordinary, such as a school-teacher. It was as good as settled.

It was a singular blow for me therefore when I began to come out very much nearer the bottom of the class than the top. My knowledge of the old subjects seemed utterly inadequate and all the new ones bewildered me. I began to be very unhappy. I wanted in particular to learn French, so that when I went to stay on my grandfather's farm I could dazzle him and whoever else might be listening by referring to the ripening wheat and the old mare in a foreign language. 'The boy's a masterpiece. Speaks French, if you'll believe me. Now let Harry hear you say, "The old nag wants a mite o' bread", in the French lingo. Go on.' That was the sort of thing I wanted to bring off. That was the point to which my so-called education had brought me. It had not only made me swollen-headed but had turned the values of things completely upside down. What I ought to have done, and I see it clearly now, was to have gone to the French master and dazzled him by saying: 'Sky looks a bit thick in the clear, master. Don't you think we ought to get that bit o' barley knocked down? We don't want to be in the cart,' which would have been much more of a foreign language to him than French was to the men in the farm.

Looking back, I see this language master very clearly now. At that time he was almost the only master left in the school: he was extremely fat and soft-fleshed and I can hear him now speaking in a voice, which grew shriller as he grew more angry. No doubt he was very clever: he had letters after his name and wore a pretty pink-lined hood to his gown on speech days. But what did he teach us? It took him weeks to make us see what we ought to have seen in a few hours.

Some of the women were even worse. Those who

were not as sour as crabs were often aggressive and ill-tempered. Anything masculine was either to be feared or despised. They, too, like the French master, taught us nothing. Only one woman, perhaps, afforded us any real education: she was a finely made but not good-looking woman, and she would stand before the class and caress her large breasts slowly backwards and forwards with her fingertips and tell us at the same time that in a right-angled triangle the sum of the squares on the two sides adjacent to the right-angle was equal to the square on the remaining side.

I begin to see now why I was so unhappy. For the first three years in that school I was not educated but repressed and the atmosphere was strained and abnormal. No doubt the war was responsible. As for my illusions, my fancies that life would be higher, different, and perhaps more aristocratic, they had all, very early on, been dissipated. Not only were there no boarders and thus no studies in which prefects would fry their midnight sausages, but we were, for the most part, the sons of lower-class people, shop-keepers, poor clergymen, shoemakers, engineers, commercial-travellers and so on, and almost all of us spoke the crude bastard dialect of that Midland district. Not that we thought of ourselves like that. The higher education had made us feel that we were very much above ourselves.

So I arrived at the fifth form and the age of fifteen without being much better off, except in self-conceit, than when I had begun. I could hardly have asked

for a bed in French, I don't think I had read a novel of
Dickens, I detested poetry, and though I could prove
Pythagoras I didn't properly know the functions of my
own body. But I was a good footballer and a fast
sprinter.

I believe I still thought of becoming a professional
footballer or a farmer or perhaps both when the war
ended and the masters began to drift back again and
replace the females. But I longed most of all to leave
the place and never see it again. I was very sensitive
and quick to be hurt, and the war-time masters and
mistresses, as though considering that a defect, seemed
to detest me.

Then, quite suddenly, a miracle took place. Going
back for the autumn term of 1919 we found that the
English mistress — a Scotswoman — had been replaced by a young infantry officer who had come home
from France without several of his fingers and with
his face atrociously mutilated and his legs and arms
stiff from wounds. He proceeded to knock us, mentally, all of a heap. Suckled at the vinegary breasts of
those repressed and impossible mistresses, we could
hardly appreciate at first his tone of quiet, almost
melancholy understanding. I remember that, as he
set us an essay on Shakespeare, he seemed very
tired. 'Don't tell me he was born in 1564. I know
that. And don't tell me he wrote *Macbeth*. I know
that too.' He treated us with extreme detachment but
with extreme kindness, and we were very much
impressed.

I particularly was impressed, and I believe I showed

it by writing an essay on Shakespeare without mentioning Shakespeare. At any rate the new master was pleased with it. Foolish as it may seem, I date my literary career from that moment. Within a few weeks I was writing my first poems and short stories, I knew a good deal of English poetry by heart, and life began suddenly to be higher and different in a way that I had never suspected. I no longer wanted to be a professional footballer, though later I very nearly became one, but an author.

Now, when I look back on the utterly useless and dreary years preceding that simple miracle, I begin to feel almost furious — furious with the repressed females with their provincialism and their petty feminine jealousies, with the school itself, its newness, its unnecessary attempts at conformation with public school standards, the constant talk of tradition and the honour and good name of the school, with the little personal tyrannies, with the examination system, with the whole complete system that enslaves masters and boys alike by its insidiously foolish rules and conventions. When I first read Shaw's jibes at the scholastic system of this country I was inclined to be shocked; not until this moment, on looking them up again, did I realize how true they are.

And so, in 1919, I began to feel my feet, or more truly my spirit. My position in the form consequently began to deteriorate and I got into the bad books of the headmaster. But I was alive and I felt extremely spirited and happy. I began to feel also an utter contempt for rules and regulations. What had I gained from them? In four years by doing as I was told and thinking as I was supposed to think, I had learned nothing. My Latin was atrocious, my French ludicrous, my chemistry quite childish. And the fault was not my own. Most of the masters, products of the same system to which I was being subjected, were hopeless, teaching by rule of thumb without a spark of intuition or imagination. They seemed disillusioned and bored, and no doubt they were underpaid. One or two of them were extremely young and undeveloped and one of them was old enough to have been my grandfather.

I see this old man very clearly now, without any effort of imagination. He was the Latin master, but at odd times he taught Scripture too. He was a short, rather portly man, with a bald head and a stiff white beard, altogether a trifle Teutonic in appearance. He was really a charming old man. He was a little deaf, he had some sort of defect, possibly a partial cataract, in one eye, and the lids of his eyes seemed to be stuck to his face by small dabs of greyish-pink putty. He suffered from indigestion and perhaps because of it he fasted once a week, I think on Thursdays, and once or twice a term he was seized with an attack of jaundice, his skin turning the sickly yellow colour of some over-ripe pear. We baited him unmercifully and inexorably, so much so that as I look back I could almost weep for the part I played in that unthinking cruelty.

There is no sort of trick known to schoolboys that we did not play on him. We used to sit occasionally with lighted candles on the seats of the desks, so that the whole room was filled with a soft effulgence and an acrid stink. I am to this day very good at blowing out a candle quickly and snuffing its smoking wick with my fingers. We translated Virgil from a common crib, making realistic mistakes and asking trickily innocent questions at the more embarrassing moments. But it was during the lessons in Holy Scripture that life became, in our eyes, worth living: for then we could derive much pleasure from asking for some greater light on the history of Bathsheba or some explanation of Saul's strange action in appropriating the foreskins of his enemies. To our minds, such is the damnable state of education in general and of sexual education in particular, all that seemed very clever.

And so I learnt nothing of Latin and very little of the richest prose in my own language, though very occasionally the beautiful sonority of the prose of Isaiah or Ruth would touch me very deeply. The old man forgave me my hopelessness at Latin, but not my neglect of the Scriptures. He saw in me, for some reason, the makings of a writer. 'Ah, Bates, Bates, you with your gifts,' he said to me once, when my marks in Scripture were no more than nine per cent and my marks in literature nearer a hundred, 'You, above all, should combine the two.' It is a sad reflection on his scholarship and his labours that that is the only thing I ever remember his having taught me.

Indeed, looking back, I don't remember anything that was taught me at that establishment of higher education, unless it is simple arithmetic, which I suppose I knew before I went there, and the foundations of what I know of English literature. Yet I passed examinations with honours, gaining illustrious commendation in subjects that have since been of not the slightest use to me and which I have now forgotten. I suppose, if I could ask them, the majority of my contemporaries there have forgotten them too. This is a strange reflection on the whole prevailing system of education, a system which, in its general tendency and effect, I think an absurd and useless one now, and which I rather think I thought just as absurd and useless fifteen years ago. At any rate when the headmaster took me aside and for almost the first time in five years spoke to me like a human being and asked me if I wouldn't seriously consider becoming a schoolmaster, I refused like a shot.

Thirty years before they had asked my father the same question. And he had answered exactly as I had done, but with the addition of a comment which does him the greatest credit. 'All very well,' he said in effect, 'but I've got my living to earn.'

I must have recalled this, consciously or unconsciously, when I also refused, and I must have had as a further reason for refusal the beginnings of my contempt for schools and scholarship. That refusal seems to me now one of the most sensible acts of my life. For at an age when I should have still have been in the sixth form I was doing something that another fifty years at the school could not have taught me; I was trying to observe and study human character and human relationships and to put my first impressions about those things on paper. In another year or two, when I might still have been under the dominion of schoolmasters disguised as professors (professing what? I sometimes wonder) I had taught myself enough about human psychology and the art of writing to be able to write my first novel and destroy it and write another. Whatever the merits of the books themselves may have been, I was free — I had escaped. I was doing at last what I wanted to do, and not, as I had been doing for so many years, what I had been told to do and what I had been told was best for me.

It was not, indeed, until I left the school that my education began.

HOT - WATER - BOTTLE LOVE

[Cheltenham Ladies' College]

BY THEODORA BENSON

I WOULD have liked it better if I had been better liked. And looking back on the year I spent there I cannot help thinking that it was nice of people to like me even as much as they did.

I had been educated at day schools so when I arrived there at the age of seventeen I was completely ignorant of boarding schools and their ways. I thought the others very queer; they thought me very queer; both sides were about right. But the staff were not queer. How they preserved their sanity coping with those battalions of girls I don't know, but they did. I suppose they must have got a lot of quiet fun out of it sometimes, but they must often have felt exasperated. Certainly it never occurred to us that they thought us funny, that we could be the objects of the mistresses' senses of humour. We supposed it to be the other way round, though I cannot recollect that we really made much fun of them. We spoke very cavalierly of most of the staff behind their backs. In their presence we would become subdued and anxious to please. Relieved of their presence, reaction would set in and we would break down into shrieks of giggling.

27

'When the sands are all dry he's as gay as a lark
And will talk in contemptuous tones of the shark,
But when the sea's in and sharks are around
His voice has a timid and tremulous sound.'

Of the ways in which I gave offence by not conforming, some come back to me as quite intolerable
and some as mere accidents for which I could not have
foreseen blame. To the latter class belongs the matter
of the bag in which I carried my books from the residential house to the College. Every other girl in my
house used a stereotyped leather bag, carrier, satchel,
or whatever it was called, costing I forget how many
shillings. I had a bag of just the same convenient
size made of matting and ornamented pictorially
with three blue geese. It was a nice bag, given to me
by a Bishop. Not only would it have been a very dull
waste of money to have bought another, but I would
then have shared everyone else's difficulty in picking
out my own bag from the mass where they were
dumped before lunch after morning school. I did
not know till several years after that my use of that
bag was taken personally and with bitterness by all.

On the other hand I had not even success to justify
my attempts to give myself *soigné* and sophisticated
airs. I have not mastered either of those attributes
since; how much less then, with ten years of conscientious labour ahead instead of behind me! Perhaps I
would have found the atmosphere of a rather silly
and gawkish finishing school in Paris more congenial.
My sister 'came out' while I was still being educated,

and my mind was on parties, clothes, cosmetics, young men, none of which I knew anything about. My sister had been very kind to me, consequently so had some of her young men. Two of these heroes had given me a cocktail at their club, fully chaperoned. The cocktail was a bronx, the club was the Wellington: dear Wellington, it is still sacred to me. And was I proud of this, or was I proud? Shortly after my arrival at Cheltenham I said to a group of girls:

'Oh, does anyone happen to remember the address of the Wellington Club? I must get this letter off to Ronnie. Grosvenor something. Really I shall be forgetting my own name next. When I think of the times that I've drunk cocktails there!'

On another occasion someone remarked that she was going to buy some vanishing cream and I called out superbly: 'Now there's a thing I could give you some useful advice about.'

The advice, very rightly, was not asked for. And this was just as well, for I had none to give.

I got my sister to give me photographs of all her young men with which to decorate my mantelpiece. My classmates behaved admirably; they never encouraged me by making any comment at all. Since those days I have so often been accused of affectation, though it comes quite naturally to me, that I shudder to think how affected I must have been at a time when I deliberately tried to lounge about with feline and filmstar grace — all elbows and Anglo-Saxon attitudes. Then on one occasion I did myself a bit of no good by telling a cowardly, flustered and futile lie. I had a few friends to tea in my room and was doing, as girls will, a crossing the channel act when the house-mistress came in at the noisiest and most displeasing bit. I muttered into the midst of an awkward silence that I had had a fit of coughing.

That I think covers their side of the matter. The rest of the things they had against me seem to me to be moot points. One sees a photograph of me and thinks that I was wrong to try and do my hair attractively. One sees a photograph of them and thinks that I was right. Then as to the question of games, I was intolerant about their heartiness and they were equally intolerant because I took all my exercise on long walks. It cancels out.

Before I go on to my side of the matter there is something that I must stress. The student of modern school literature who expects the stuff to be served up really hot is going to be disappointed. We were almost incredibly innocent. Most of us were eighteen or nineteen, a few of us seventeen or even twenty. I believe that hardly anyone knew what are so exclusively called THE facts of life. Even I was among the more knowing. One of the girls once asked me how babies came. I had a sort of hazy idea but was not very sure of my ground, so I benevolently answered that I thought I should only embarrass both of us by telling her. The usual rules and regulations which belong to the residential section of girls' schools were to us quite silly and meaningless. I think our childish ignorance was almost excessive, and that we might have been a little less foolish if we had known a little more. But I cannot find that this innocence did any of us any harm. All of us that I have come across since have turned out as normal as can be.

It being understood that they were all very nice, very harmless young ladies, I must admit that I had every excuse for being amazed and disgusted at their capacity for heroine worship. I had heard of little girls having tiresome devotions to older ones, of older girls adoring some particular mistress. At my kindergarten I had myself so admired the scripture mistress as to paint her Christmas cards all the year round of holly and plum puddings or of the birth of Christ, and to send her shoe boxes full of flowers. I had sometimes loved the little boys, generally getting engaged to them and on one occasion knocking out a rival for the sake of my simpering small hero. But I simply did not know until I went to Cheltenham Ladies' College that one grown girl could dote to idolatry upon another girl of her own age. These affections, known in the College as 'raves', had all the emotional aspects of calf love or the flutters between a young man and a maid. It seemed kind of odd to me.

They were painful, these raves, and tearful, and, since the College was the world to us who lived therein, they were for the time being important. The ravers would give the ravees anonymous presents of cakes and sweets, and then look conscious. They would be in heaven if accorded a smile as their inamoratas passed them in a passage. They would entreat me to snoop round the bedrooms and spy out who held converse with who. Generally the beloveds loathed it, but sometimes they were touched or flattered at the beginning, encouraged their admirers, then found the thing palled woefully, and got landed in a pretty how do you do of scenes and recriminations. Since I had never been to a boarding school before, these ecstasies were beyond my reach, though I did once unexpectedly find myself a snake in the grass, playing in fact that well-known role the false female friend.

What endless discussions of tactics and strategy we used to hold after supper! I still think I gave very good advice to those love-lorn maidens on how to deal with each other. But whenever the advice happened to be 'Hold off for a bit', like many wiser and older they couldn't take it. One of my afflicted friends I think bound all raves into a nutshell when she said to me:

'It's so heartless to like Patsy better than me, when you think how I filled her hot-water-bottle for her every night of the winter term. I don't think Patsy would have filled her hot-water-bottle for her every night — at least I'm sure she wouldn't have done it in quite the same way.'

The other thing I still hold against my fellow students is that they used at breakfast not only to smell their perfectly good boiled eggs, but to pass them round the tables for their friends to smell and pass opinions on too.

Girls *en masse* are quite apt to produce that morbid atmosphere of raves and there is nothing the authorities can do about it. I have a deep distrust of hero or heroine worship in any walk of life. I dislike anything that tends to make people substitute emotion for reason as a regular thing, or to lose themselves in the luxury of hanging on to something else, or to make another human being their brain or their conscience. I would rather see them standing on their own feet and choosing wrong than being towed along in the right direction. Anything of the rave nature always strikes me as unhealthy. But the raves of my school-fellows were no more than a phase of growing up. They were of no significance in the post-College life of the girls. 'They came and went and are not, and come no more anew.' There was nothing sinister about them. We must all be silly sometimes and that was the revolting way a little passing silliness took my contemporaries at College.

The egg business, of course, is inexcusable.

In trying to recapture the atmosphere of my school days and give an account of Cheltenham Ladies' College, I have only been able to talk of myself and my school-fellows. For when it comes to the organiza-tion of the College and the residential houses, and to the teaching, I have nothing that is not pleasant and efficient to report and who wants to read about that? I will get it over very quickly. The food, with the exception of one pudding which we got about twice in three weeks made of liquid blancmange and something tasting like dog biscuits, was excellent. It was good, plentiful, nice and varied. The accommodation was all we could wish. We were allowed a fair degree of liberty. There were parts of the town where we could go alone, and we could visit most of it if we went two or three together. Two or three together could go long walks or bicycle expeditions into the country. There were places that were out of bounds, among them not unreasonably the race course, the polo ground and the boys' college football ground, but this I fortunately did not discover till two-thirds of the way through my time there so I was not greatly inconvenienced. Prayers were short, and involved a nice bit of hymn singing. Only one church service was compulsory on Sundays. We had a grand library at the College and a fair amount of time for browsing in it. The teaching was so stimulating and good that most of us felt inspired to read quite a lot of good stuff we needn't have read at all. My house mistress was kindness itself to me. I remember with great respect and affection both the head of my class room and the Principal of the College, while one of my teachers was among the most interesting, intelligent and delightful women that I have ever met. For the first time in my life I worked hard and enjoyed work. And though I forgot everything I'd learnt within a month of leaving for good, I have always thought that it is better to have known and forgotten than never to have known at all.

I began by saying that had I been more popular I should have been happier at Cheltenham. I think this is true. During my last term I had a few established friendships and I think I was happier. Though I passed through another tiresome stage then, natural this time rather than affected, a sort of Madcap-

Molly-the-Pride-of-the-Fourth business which would, had I been in a book, have made me very popular but which in actual fact made no difference either way. I got up sweepstakes on horse races, and brought out a ribald newspaper which was instantly suppressed.

It is such fun reminiscing. When I visited Cheltenham again, years after, with a friend who knew it not, I had so lovely a time recounting anecdotes, showing her round, telling her the nicknames for this place and that place, pointing out where we bought cream buns and sugar biscuits at eleven o'clock in the black and white marble corridor, that were I given to kidding myself in that sort of way I could easily have made the preposterous announcement that my school days had been the happiest time of my life. Really that week-end of revisiting the old haunts and meeting again the old friends, acquaintances and enemies was wholly delightful. There were my fellow students looking pretty and nicely dressed, talking amusingly and sanely. It seemed incredible. What was so particularly strange was to be at Cheltenham with all the same people and not to find them completely and utterly humourless.

As regards humour they compelled my respect and my gratitude. I had put a school in my first novel, a hash-up of every school that I had ever heard anything about, much of the material borrowed from my own school and all of it guyed. I felt some embarrassment at facing all the Cheltonians, but they scored off me. I think the school in that novel very funny. I was not surprised that the staff of Cheltenham thought it funny and congratulated me cordially; they must often have wanted to say the same things. But I was surprised that my fellow students, many of whom were most obviously ragged in this novel, thought it a very funny and entirely justifiable joke. I even felt a little humbled!

I have related, perhaps too incoherently, all that I remember of my year at Cheltenham. All the bad, which seems slight and ludicrous; all the good, which seems sufficient and solid. The fact remains that I disliked my time there on the whole, and that not only did I, the fish out of water, dislike my school days, but that many of the others, in spite of conforming to type, of being used to schools, of playing games, of having *esprit de corps*, disliked it or were more or less unhappy.

But many modern writers make out that schools, and unhappiness at schools, have dire effects on the characters and futures of the pupils. It just isn't so. People don't grow up warped or embittered or the victims of complexes because they had a few good cries in the cloakroom or somebody once snubbed them. I know quite well that my own character is my own fault, and I'd rather have it that way than push the responsibility on to my upbringing. At sixteen I was happy, from seventeen to twenty I was fairly unhappy, from twenty on I grew steadily happier, and now — let me put it on record while it lasts — I am very happy. I should be the same me whether I had been to Cheltenham or not, and if I ever try to blame anything concerning me off on to the old school I shall be a liar.

36

THE MULBERRY TREE

[Downe House]

BY ELIZABETH BOWEN

THE house with a shallow front lawn, swagged in July with Dorothy Perkins roses, stood back from a tarmac road outside the Kentish village of Downe. The main block, three stories high, had a white pillared portico and a dado of ivy, looking friendly and undistinguished. It contained classrooms and bedrooms for about sixty girls, the staff study and the dining-room. To the left facing the porch (as we seldom had time to do) was a stable-yard, to the right, a warren of painted iron buildings — gymnasium, music-rooms, wash-rooms — twisted off at an angle, parallel with the road. A low trellis of ivy concealed these windows.

The back of the house, one portion curving out in a deep bay, faced a lawn flanked each side by heavily treed paths, tunnels in summer. A bed of azaleas outside the senior study french window made the summer term exotic. Features of this lawn landscape were an old mulberry tree with an iron belt and a mound with a large ilex, backed by evergreen shrubs, on which Shakespeare plays were acted. It was usual during rehearsals to pluck and chew the leaves of the ilex tree. We girls were for ever masticating some foreign substance, leaves of any kind, grass from the playing

37

fields, paper, india rubber, splinters from pencil-ends or the hems of handkerchiefs. In the course of my three years at school both the ilex and mulberry trees took on an emotional significance; under the mulberry a friend whose brother at that time captained the Winchester eleven, and who was herself our only over-hand bowler, criticized my behaviour on an occasion, saying I had done something that was not cricket. The lawn gave on a meadow crossed by a path to the playing field: beyond the school boundary, meadows and copses rolled off into Kent pleasantly. In summer there was a great smell of hay. I remember also one June a cuckoo that used to flap round the school roof, stout, squawking and losing its mystery. It has taken years for me to reinstate cuckoos. The Cudham valley was said to be a great place for nightingales, but we girls can never have walked there at the right time. . . . From across country, features of this rather odd and imposing back view of the house were its very white window-frames, a glass veranda on to which the drawing-room debouched and a modern addition, one side, in the form of a kind of chalet, from whose balcony I played Jezebel with a friend's teddy bear.

The survival of such childish inanimate pets was encouraged by fashion; several dormitory beds with their glacial white quilts were encumbered all day and shared nightly with rubbed threadbare teddy bears, monkeys or in one case a blue plush elephant. Possibly this seemed a good way to travesty sentiment: we cannot really have been idiotic girls. A friend of mine wore a carved ivory Chinese dog round her neck on a gold cord for some days, then she was asked to wear this inside her djibbah. A good deal of innocent fetishism came to surround these animals; the mistress of the blue elephant used to walk the passages saying: 'You must kiss my elephant.' Photos of relatives, sometimes quite distant but chosen for their good appearance, the drawings of Dulac, Medici prints and portraits of Napoleon, Charles I, Rupert Brooke, Sir Roger Casement or Mozart lent advertising touches of personality to each cubicle's walls, slung on threads from the frieze-rail and flapping and tapping in an almost constant high wind from the open windows. The ever difficult business of getting oneself across was most pressing of all at this age: restricted possessions, a uniform dictated down to the last detail and a self-imposed but rigid emotional snobbishness shutting the more direct means of self-expression away. Foibles, mannerisms we therefore exaggerated most diligently.

If anyone said 'You are always so such-and-such' one felt one had formed a new intimacy and made one's mark. A good many young women were led to buffoon themselves. It seemed fatal not to be at least one thing to excess, and if I could not be outstandingly good at a thing I preferred to be outstandingly bad at it. Personality came out in patches, like damp through a wall.

The dormitories were called bedrooms, and we had little opinion of schools where the bedrooms were called dormitories. Ours were in fact the bedrooms of a fair-sized country house, divided into from four to six cubicles. The window cubicles went to the best people, who were sometimes terribly cold at nights; the door cubicle went to the youngest inhabitant, who could hold everyone up if her sense of decency were over-acute. 'You *can't* come through' she would shout; 'I am indecent.' The niceties of curtain-drawing and of intrusion varied from bedroom to bedroom, according to temper, but we always closed our curtains to say our prayers. No embarrassment surrounded the saying of prayers at this school; in fact it would have been more embarrassing to have left them unsaid. Whom one sleeps with is always rather important, and ill-assorted companions could cast a gloom over the term. There was always one rather quiet girl who patently wished herself elsewhere, lurked a good deal behind her curtains and was afraid to speak. As in a railway carriage, one generally disliked one's companions less after some time. The tone of a bedroom would be, of course, set by the noisiest girl, who talked most freely about her private affairs. As one began to realize that bedroom lists for a term were drawn up on a psychological basis, the whole thing became more interesting. Great friends were not put together and we were not allowed into each other's bedrooms, but it was always possible to stand and talk in the door, with one toe outside. Assignations for serious or emotional talks connected themselves with the filling of hot-water-bottles and water cans at a tap outside the bathrooms, when one was otherwise ready for bed. Girls of a roving disposition with a talent for intimacy were always about this passage. A radiator opposite this tap was in demand in winter; one could lean while one talked and warm the spine through the dressing-gown. The passage was dim-lit, with wobbly gas brackets, and it was always exciting to see who had got there first. The radiator was near the headmistress's door, and she would disperse any group she came out and found. It irritated her to see us being girlish in any way. We cannot really have been emotional girls; we were not highly sexed and any attractions had an aesthetic, snobbish, self-interested tinge. Conversations over the radiator were generally about art, Roman Catholicism, suicide, or how impossible somebody else had been. At nine o'clock a bell rang from the matron's room and we all darted back to our bedrooms and said our prayers.

I first went to this school in September 1914. We unpacked our trunks in a cement passage outside the gymnasium and carried our things upstairs. The school must have re-assembled with an elating sense of emergency, but as I was new I was not conscious of this. Everything seemed so odd that the war was dwarfed, and though one had been made to feel that one was now living in history, one's own biography was naturally more interesting. I found my school-fellows rather terse and peremptory, their snubbing of me had a kind of nobility: whether this arose from the war's or my own newness I did not ask: as I had been told that this was a very good school it was what I had been led to expect. A squad of troops marching past in the dark on the tarmac road, whistling, pointed the headmistress's address to us in the gymnasium that first night of term. Wind kept flapping the window cords on their pulleys, the gas jets whistled and the girls drawn up by forms in resolute attitudes looked rather grim. The headmistress stated that it did not matter if we were happy so long as we were good. At my former school the headmistress had always said she knew we should be good as long as we were happy. That sounded sunnier. But in my three years at this school I learnt to define happiness as a kind of inner irrational exaltation having little to do with morals one way or the other. That night in the gymnasium I felt some apprehension that my character was to be lopped, or even forcibly moulded, in this place, but this came to be dispelled as the term wore on. The war having well outlasted my schooldays, I cannot imagine a girls' school without a war. The moral stress was appalling. We grew up under the intolerable obligation of being fought for, and could not fall short in character without recollecting that men were dying for us. During my second year, the *Daily Mail* came out with its headline about food-hogs, and it became impossible to eat as much as one wished, which was to over-eat, without self-consciousness. If the acutest food shortage had already set in, which it had not, meals would really have been easier. As it was, we *could* over-eat, but it became unfeeling to do so. The war dwarfed us and made us morally uncomfortable, and we could see no reason why it should ever stop. It was clear, however, that someone must have desired it, or it would not have begun. In my first term, we acted a pageant representing the

Allies for the headmistress's birthday, and later sang
songs of the epoch, such as 'We don't want to lose you,
but . . .' at a concert in the village, in our white
muslin Saturday evening frocks. Most eligible fighters
had, however, by this time gone to the war and we can
only have made their relatives more hysterical. An
excellent bun supper was provided by the village
committee, and some of us over-ate.

I do not remember ever discussing the war among
ourselves at school. Possibly some of the girls may
have done so, but I had a sense of inferiority owing to
having no brothers and not taking in a daily paper.
Though, seated beside one of the staff at meals one
would say: 'Aren't the French doing splendidly?'
or 'Isn't it awful about the Russians?' The Danish
music mistress, however, had melancholia and we were
not allowed to mention the war at her table. I do not
think it was so much the war that made her melan-
cholic as her unhappy friendship with the violin
mistress; any attempt to make conversation with her
was the last straw. She looked extraordinarily like
Hamlet, and as she was a neutral I always resented
her taking up this attitude about the war. . . . If a
girl's brother were killed or wounded we were all too
much embarrassed to speak of it. Though death
became familiar, it never became less awkward: if
heroic feeling ran low in us I think this was
because the whole world's behaviour seemed to be
travestying our own: everywhere, everyone was be-
having as we were all, at our ages, most anxious not to
behave. Things were being written and said constantly

43

that would have damned any one of us: the world seemed to be bound up in a tragic attack of adolescence and there seemed no reason why we should ever grow up, since moderation in behaviour became impossible. So we became in contradistinction violently precious, martyrized by our own good taste. Our morbidity was ingrowing. I cannot, either, remember discussing men. Possibly the whole sex had gloomy associations. One or two of the girls fell in love in the holidays, but something in the atmosphere made it impossible to talk of this naturally without seeming at once to make copy of it. All the same, I and my friends all intended to marry early, partly because this appeared an achievement or way of making one's mark, also from a feeling it would be difficult to settle to anything else until this was done. (Like passing the School Certificate.) Few of my friends anticipated maternity with either interest or pleasure, and though some have since become mothers it still seems inappropriate. Possibly, however, we were not natural girls. We may have discussed love, but I do not remember how. The future remained very hazy and insecure. We were not ambitious girls, though we all expected to distinguish ourselves in some way. Not one of us intended to be L.O.P.H. (Left On Pa's Hands). We lived, however, intensively in the present; when the present became over-powering there was an attic-loft over the bedroom ceilings in the main buildings, with sacks and a cistern in it, where an enterprising person could go and weep. Less fastidious people wept in their cubicles.

We were not in love with each other at all continuously, or, as far as I know, with the staff at all. A certain amount of emotion banked up in the holidays, when letters became important. During the school day we all looked violently plain: school uniform, even djibbahs, cannot expect to suit everyone; red wrists stuck out of our cuffs and our hair (short hair was not at that time the prevailing fashion) was so skinned back that our eyes would hardly shut. After games we charged indoors, stripped, rubbed down, put on stays and private clothes, released our front hair and became a little more personable. On Saturday nights, in modified evening dresses, quite a certain amount of glamour set in. In the week, curvilinear good looks were naturally at a discount and a swaggering, nonchalant air cut the most ice. If you were not good at games the best way of creating an atmosphere was to be good at acting. We acted a good deal. On Saturday afternoons, one or two people who could play the piano emotionally had séances in the music rooms. All this was the best we could put up in the way of romance. All the same, one or two people contrived to keep diaries, moon round the garden alone and be quite unhappy.

Competitive sociability and team spirit was rather well united at my school by the custom of picking up tables. The first day of term seven seniors shut themselves up and, by rotative bidding, each picked up from the rest of the school a team of about eight for her table at meals. Each team moved round each week to the next of the seven dining-room tables, each table presided over by one of the staff. The object of each team was to make the most conversation possible, and to be a success: girls were therefore picked with a view to chattiness, desirability, tact, table manners, resource and charm. Certain unfortunate girls were never in demand, and the screams of seniors repudiating them could sometimes be heard from the other end of the garden. It was a great thing to be at the head of the most patently animated table in the dining-room. Many of us have grown up to be good hostesses. If a girl sat just eating on without saying anything the head of the table would kick at her, if within reach. So that young nervous girls got into a way of saying almost anything. The great thing was to amuse the mistress whose table it was, and keep her smiling constantly: each girl had to take it in turns to do this. There was a French table and a German table: the games mistress was usually difficult to talk to. The headmistress sometimes received our remarks with irony, and was inclined to say 'Quite . . .' The table rule bound us only for breakfast and dinner; at tea and supper we sat with whom we liked, few of the staff were present and very merry we were. Quarrels, if any, sometimes occurred at this time.

The other great social occasion was Saturday evening (as I have said). We danced (we thought) rather glamorously in the gymnasium to a piano, and dances were often booked up some days ahead. On summer Saturday evenings we walked round the garden between dances, feeling unlike ourselves. The garden was long, with lime trees and apple trees and long grass with cuckoo flowers in it: it looked very beautiful in the late evening light, with the sound of the piano coming out through the gymnasium door. On winter Saturday evenings we danced more heartily, in order to keep warm. The staff filed in in evening dresses and sat on a platform, watching the dancing, and occasionally being asked to dance, with expressions of animation which, now that I look back, command my respect.

Lessons must have occupied a good deal of our time, but I remember very little of this. What I learnt seems to have been absorbed into my system, which shows how well taught I was. I used to sit riveting, or trying to rivet, the mistress's eye, but must otherwise have been pretty passive. I spent an inordinate amount of time over the preparation for some lessons; the rest of my preparation time went by in reading poetry or the Bible or looking up more about the facts of life in the *Encyclopaedia Britannica*. We were morbidly honourable girls and never spoke to each other at preparation or in our bedrooms after the lights were out. I often wonder whether in after life one has not suffered from an overstrained honour from having been too constantly put upon it in youth, and whether the espionage one hears of in foreign schools might not have kept one's sense of delinquency more enduringly active. In these ways, we were almost too good to last. We did not pass notes either, though one of my friends, just back from a day in London, once wrote on the margin of her rough note book, and pushed across to me, that Kitchener had been drowned. Perhaps the occasion may have excused the breach. I simply thought, however, that she was pulling my leg . . . Games were compulsory and took up the afternoon: it did not matter being bad at them so long as you showed energy. At lacrosse, girls who could run would pound up and down the field; those who could not gripped their crosses fiercely and stalked about. Lacrosse is such a fierce game that I wonder we all lived through it. Hockey, though ungainly, is not nearly so perilous. The only real farce was cricket, a humiliating performance for almost all. I never thought worse of anyone for being good at games so long as she was not unattractive in other ways; one or two of the games committee had, however, an air of having no nonsense about them that was depressing. We were anything but apathetic about matches: when a match was played away the returning team would, if victorious, begin to cheer at a given turn of the road; we all sat with straining ears; if the charabanc rolled up in silence we knew the worst. Our team so often won that I should like to think we had given them moral support.

The literary society was presided over by the head-mistress, of whom I should like to place it on grateful record that she did definitely teach me how not to write. There were gardens to garden in, if you had nothing more personal to do in your spare time, and, because of the war, there was haymaking in season. Two or three of the girls who had formed the idea that they wished to be engineers in after life spent a good deal of time looking in through the windows of the engine room at the light plant and water-pumping machine; sometimes they were let in by the geography mistress to help her oil the thing. The geography mistress was a Pole, who had built the chapel as well as all the other modern additions to the school. The chapel was put up during my second year and dedicated by the Bishop of Rochester: a friend of mine pointed out to me during the service that the Bishop's sleeves were not white but of very pale pink lawn, and I have had no opportunity since to correct this impression: perhaps it was not incorrect. The chapel was approached by a dark, draughty and rather impressive arcade from the gymnasium. There were no cases of religious mania or any other obsession while I was at school.

Seeing *Mädchen in Uniform*, and reading more sensitive people's impressions of their school life, makes me feel that either my old school was prosaic or that I was insensitive. A toughish, thick child, I did not in fact suffer in any way. My vanity would have been mortified anywhere and my heart was at that age really all over the place. At my old school there was nothing particular to conform to, and the worst that can be said of it is that I got no kick out of not conforming to anything. I was only too well understood, and when I left school my relations complained that my personality had made rapid and rank growth. I talked too much with a desperate self-confidence induced perhaps by competitive talking at meals. I say with deference to the susceptibilities of possible other essayists in this book that I consider my old school an exceedingly good one. If girls ought really to be assembled and taught, I can think of no better way of assembling and teaching them. No one dragooned us; in the course of three years I never once heard the expression *esprit de corps* and we were never addressed as future mothers. The physical discomfort was often extreme but (I am prepared to believe now that its details escape me) salutary. I regret that my palate has been blunted for life by being made to finish up everything on my plate, so that when I dine out with a gourmet my manner becomes exceedingly artificial. I was taught not only how not to write (though I still do not always write as I should) but how not, if possible, to behave, and how not to exhibit feeling. I have not much idea what more than ten people at my school were like, so cannot well generalize about our type or mentality. No one of my companions betrayed my affections, corrupted me, aggravated my inferiority complex, made me wish I had more money, gave me a warp for life or did anything that is supposed to happen at schools. There is nothing I like better than feeling one of a herd, and after a term or two I began to feel firmly stuck in.

Memory is, as Proust has it, so oblique and selective that no doubt I see my school days through a subjective haze. I cannot believe that those three years were idyllic: days and weeks were no doubt dreary and squalid on end. I recall the most thundering disappointments and baulked ambitions, but those keep repeating themselves throughout after life. I do not desire to live those three years again, but I should be exceedingly sorry to have them cut out of my past. Some years after I left, the house, after so much pounding and trampling, began to wear out; the school moved and the building has been reinstated as some kind of shrine, for Charles Darwin lived there for some years and died there, I believe, too. Our Morris wall-papers have been all stripped off and the white woodwork grained: the place now rather seriously and unsatirically reconstructs a late Victorian epoch. Our modern additions have been pulled down; the geography mistress has re-erected the chapel, the gymnasium, the lavatories and the music-rooms elsewhere. When I revisited the place, only the indestructible cement flooring of these remained. To indulge sentiment became almost impossible. I have never liked scientific people very much, and it mortifies me to think of them trampling reverently around there on visiting days, thinking of Charles Darwin and ignorant of my own youth.

LANGY ROAD

[A Salford Council School]

BY WALTER GREENWOOD

My Salford school days were brief because of economic and domestic circumstances which need to be mentioned.

Maternal ambition was responsible for my enrolment at the Langworthy Road Council School where a 'better class' of boy was reputed to attend. In the ordinary course of events I would have been pitchforked into the handiest council school. But my mother was a remarkable woman.

She was her father's daughter, and he was a grammar-school boy, a man of iron will, a strict disciplinarian and a Socialist in the movement's earliest days. He had a large family and, because of his views and independent nature, he was an unpopular man. Consequently he suffered. So that my mother, the eldest of the large family, was forced into the mill at a very early age. She read Shakespeare by the loom-side: she walked from Pendleton to Manchester, three miles, and back again, twice and thrice weekly, and after a long day at the mill, to spend her coppers at the opera. Contrary to her father's strong advice she married the interesting and irresponsible man who was my father.

He was a Card, a hairdresser by profession and an

53

operatic singer by inclination. Despite the fact that he never had a singing lesson in his life, I have yet to hear, speaking comparatively, a richer bass; and I have heard the best. He carried his clothes magnificently but he could not carry his liquor. Spasmodically he indulged heavily and I have vivid recollections of witnessing his signature to The Pledge to abstain from alcohol. Indeed, I think I still have some of the Temperance Society's cards testifying to his vow. Much can be forgiven him, for his, like mine, was a brutalized childhood.

Thinking to reform him, my mother persuaded him to move from a slum shop in which I was born to a shop in a better neighbourhood. Across the way was the School, then ten years old. I was five.

Frequently my father's excesses produced the inevitable financial crises. I distinctly remember coming home from school on the first day to find a strange man sitting at the beautiful carved walnut table which was my mother's pride. The man was drinking tea from the best china. And he was eating Seed Cake. I was very interested in the latter. I can see the glass cake-stand, the lace doily and the cake. The man looked at me, I at him, but he did not offer me a piece. He was the bailiff.

Our removal from this shop to another, back in the slums again, was effected with the aid of a bassinet. The streets were wet that night. I still see the silhouettes of my parents trudging in the darkness, neither speaking.

My father again signed The Pledge.

At this period I was a scholar in the Infants' Department. This section comprised a large hall with class-rooms either side. There was a Maypole in the centre of the hall round which we danced. But the hall's most important item of furnishing was a glass-fronted cabinet wherein was set a desert scene: miniature palm trees, sands, lions, tigers and camels whose heads, on springs, nodded solemnly if the cabinet was surreptitiously pushed.

We practised handwriting on trays of sand. Our punishment for wrongdoing was to be sent to solitary confinement, just where I forget.

I can remember being punished in this manner. With it I associate a cellar, though I will not be sure. I remember, with certainty, being banished from the Infants' Department to this solitary confinement and being forgotten by the teacher. Noon came and the other children were freed. The staff departed to their homes until two o'clock. I remained in my exile, alone, wondering, whimpering. After an hour and a half the children began to dribble back. At two o'clock schooling was renewed.

My mother appeared, distraught. Where was I? The teacher remembered. I was found. Profuse apologies in front of the large audience of interested children. Later in the afternoon I was grudgingly permitted to return to the school.

Meanwhile my father had practised his trade on my hair. It was brushed and parted beautifully. And all the little girls offered to make room for me on their desks after the headmistress had paraded me as an

55

example of neatness. This episode with another, when my ear stopped a snowball as I watched a snowfight between the Big Boys, is all that remains of the Infants' Department. In the whole of my school career I never won a prize or an attendance certificate. I simply was not interested. Probably the fault was the teachers'; likely enough, much of it was mine. To me, the Old School was a place to be avoided, a sort of punishment for being young.

Every July, before the summer holidays, the whole of the school shuddered at the prospect of 'th' exam.'; or, as most us called it, 'the eggs, ham and bacon'. New pen-nibs were distributed, new blotting-paper, spotless foolscap sheets. And the hot July afternoons heard nothing but the scratchings of pens or heads. To pass the examination meant promotion to a higher 'standard'. Classes were named from Standard I to Standard VII. There were no Forms.

I question very much whether Nature could have produced a more provocative set of boys than those who grew up with me. It was not we who were driven mad by such subjects as mental arithmetic, but the teachers. One of them, a small, knock-kneed man who we nicknamed 'Bandy', used to collapse impotently across his desk at the answers received to such problems of a man and a half who ate a cake and a half in a day and a half. He would cover his eyes with his hands and moan 'Donkeys', then bawl, glaring, 'Thickheaded, good-for-nothing louts', and cover his eyes again. Then, while we were chuckling at his anger we, unaware that he was peeping at us through

56

his fingers, would suddenly find ourselves named.
He was vicious in punishing. We were called out in
front of the class, made to extend our palms while
he lashed at them savagely with a thin cane.

Sometimes our teachers had cause to leave the
room. Without exception each teacher of my knowledge set the class on its honour not to misbehave
itself during his absence. He would depart and shut
the door after him. A surge of restlessness would hiss
round the room; fugitive strains from a mouth organ,
thrummings of a jew's harp; the squashy smack of an
ink-sodden piece of blotting paper as it hit Claude
—— (who used to scream with fear when thunder
was in the air) on the neck; the laughter of Billy ——
as he put his catapult away. Then somebody would
dare Bob to drain the inkwell, and, to the huge delight
of all, Bob would raise the inkwell, pour the ink down
his throat, then put out his black tongue to show that
there was no trickery. Somebody would punch
somebody else in the back or kick somebody's shin
with the cool request to 'Pass it on'. So that while 'it'
was going the rounds chaos ensued. And when pande-
monium was at its height the door would open, and the
teacher, sneering, would enter to deliver a weighty
oration on his contempt for our honour.

The teachers' disgust for us was only equalled by our
disgust for them, and for the School. There was nothing at all of the Harrow-and-Eton Alma Mater
affection. The handbell knelled us to imprisonment
at 9 a.m. and 2 p.m. We were released at noon and
4.30 p.m.

Not infrequently revolt against the insufferable tedium found expression in playing truant, or 'wag' as we called it. There were a number of boys always willing to set authority at defiance. Tom, Billy, Harry, Bob and myself. Tom was an ornithologist, Billy a born fighter, Harry the swimmer and Bob the daring. I was flattered to be permitted their company on illicit escapades.

Of all our adventurings one lovely remembrance lingers still. We had 'wagged it' one sunny June morning. We had spent an hour chasing and riding a flock of sheep in a field. A policeman chased us away, and, presently, we found ourselves in Bluebell Woods, where now is a council estate. Here used to be a farm and rich meadow land. The other boys disappeared, nesting in the hedges, doubtless. I was left alone in the sunlight. Warm winds breathed in my face. I could see the heat haze shimmering in the meadow, the drunken flight of butterflies; birds warbled unseen and the drowsy hum of the bees urged me to lie down. I lay drinking it all in and stroking the grasses because they all seemed to conspire to make me happy.

Then all was shattered. A crackling in the hedge, the bursting out of my mates with Daddy Thompson's, the farmer's, one-eyed dog at their heels. As we went home I was sickened at the prospect of the School on the morrow and the grey streets to which I had to return. I was always afraid of punishment as a child, particularly of the deferred variety. How many strokes of the cane we got for that escapade I do not know. I know that I sometimes kept a secret and solitary tryst with the meadow. But I don't remember ever again catching it in such a gracious mood: either rain was falling or the sky overcast or the season changed.

Change, change, a melancholy word.

Coming from school one day I found great crowds choking the streets about the shop in which we lived. The shop door was shut. On my appearance the people stopped talking to look at me. Embarrassed, I rattled the latch. An aunt opened the door but wouldn't let me in. 'Go and play,' she said. Then one of the street boys who belonged to the same 'gang' as myself pushed forward and informed me, eagerly: 'Your pa's dead.'

I don't know that the news had much effect on me except to make me feel rather important. Sympathetic women in shawls who stood in the street weeping in testimony of my father's immense popularity, gave me halfpennies. I too became immensely popular with the urchin crowd.

My mother, my sister and myself were left entirely without provision. My mother secured work as a waitress: we removed from the shop to a poky hole of a place and settled down once again. The economics of this period should be of interest. I was nine years old when my father died, my sister four years my junior. My mother earned twelve shillings a week plus lunch and tea. We were relieved to the extent of eight shillings a week by the Board of Guardians. This amount was reduced to half a crown when, later,

I obtained spare-time work. So the present Means Test is not an innovation.

Duty kept my mother from home until eight or nine at night. During the day my sister and I were left to fend for ourselves. There was a pastry-cook's at the corner of the street where we ran up a weekly bill. During summertime, when the narrow streets were suffocating, it was our habit to dine *al fresco*. With cups of tea and such sweet cake as we could cajole from the shopkeeper, Betty and I would sit on the w.c. roof, munch, sip, converse with friends in the street, and sometimes extend invitations to them to join us by clambering up the backyard wall.

In winter it was different. We tried to out-dawdle each other on the way home from school. To be first home meant having to light the fire. Winter was to be dreaded. After morning school the fire would just be warming the room when the clock would warn us of school once again.

Our income, need I say, was grossly inadequate. My mother had to find extra work. In celebrating something or other there can always be an excuse found for boozing and gluttony. Consequently, such affairs as civic and Masonic banquets which began late and were continued into the small hours afforded more work for my mother. Food, too, sometimes. I was an eater of broken meats at an early age: of necessity, not choice.

It was the habit of us two children to retire to bed and for me to tie a string round my ankle and to dangle the string's other end through the bedroom window. At two or three a.m. I would be wakened by tugs at the string, stumble down stairs half asleep to unbolt the door. Work for her and school for us next day.

Then began another aspect of education quite neglected by the School. My mother, as I have said, was passionately devoted to opera. She came home one evening excited with news that the Beecham Opera Company had made their headquarters in the building where her café was. Instantly she became popular with the artistes and was the flattered recipient of many complimentary tickets. By the time I was twelve there was scarcely an operatic air which I couldn't name. From that I graduated to the Free Trade Hall and the Hallé concerts.

War.

Banquets were abandoned from motives of patriotism. The extra shillings ceased. I found a spare-time job with a milk-roundsman of an early morning; in the evenings I delivered newspapers for a man with a barber's shop who had served his time under my father. I was given this job out of sympathy, and the man's affection for me proved to be so great that after I had delivered the newspapers, he used to keep me lathering his customers and sweeping his shop until closing-time — without pay.

One day some military men created great excitement by appearing at the 'Langy Road' school. Some days later us older boys were excused classes to assist in moving articles of a portable nature to another council school not far away. The school was to be a military hospital.

School hours were changed surprisingly. Factory idiom was introduced to the time-table. There were to be two 'shifts'. The original scholars of the other school were to attend from 8.30 a.m. till 10.30 and from 1 p.m. till 3 p.m. The hours appointed for us of 'Langy Road' were 10.30 a.m. until 1 p.m.; 3 p.m. until 5 p.m. Quite a number of the boys of the seventh standard then romping in the schoolyard were to die in the Dardanelles.

The two schools despised each other. We were regarded by the others as interlopers. Our hostility and contempt for them was unconcealed. In those days it was customary for the school's best fighter to carry the title 'cock o' the school'. He held the name while he was prepared to defend, successfully, his title against all comers. Billy was our man. And since his family, like mine, was fatherless and also in poor circumstances, a vague affinity existed between us. Nobody tried to bully me while Billy was within call. No sooner were we, as a school, installed in our new home than challenges were exchanged.

The 'cock' of the other school, a hefty, rough-looking boy arranged to meet our man after five o'clock. Both schools, yelling, attended the assigned place. I cannot relate the details since I was unable to maintain a front place. All I remember was being crushed and pushed, swaying with the crowd and yelling until I was hoarse. Finally the crowd broke, Billy, fists clenched, flushed, panting, an eye half-shut, flashed by, carried shoulder-high. The vanquished lay alone, blubbering in the mud. I felt most miserable to see him.

At this period breadwinners were being recruited by the score. Our income at home was shrunk to an irreducible minimum. Other families were in a similar predicament. A boom began in the pawn-broking business. Running home from school one day I saw a notice in a pawnshop window: 'BOY WANTED'. I got the job. The hours were 6.30 a.m. of a Monday morning until school-time at 10.30, then 6 p.m. until closing time; 8 p.m. weekdays, 9 Saturdays, other than Monday the shop opened at 8 a.m. Wages 3s. 6d. a week. A windfall.

As I hated school so I hated the shop. I cursed my impulsiveness. But there was nothing to be done about it. Even with the extra three and sixpence we could not manage. How on earth my mother managed to keep out of debt is a mystery.

School became a sort of inconvenient necessity, a place which one was forced to attend, an interruption in the earning of a livelihood. Perhaps this explains why I have so little to say about it. All was mean and shabby and without colour. Sooty school, smoky streets, the trudge homewards to the cold house and empty grate. A swig of tea, a bite of such food as was in the house, then to the pawnbroker's until closing time. While, irrelevant as it may seem, millions of pounds daily were being spent in the destruction of human life.

Subconsciously I was being educated, at least, pre-paring to be educated. It was not until years later that the study of Marxian economics satisfactorily ex-plained the causes of my predicament. Accidentally I discovered a number of pamphlets which had belonged to my grandfather; but much rain was to fall on Manchester and Salford before I made the discovery.

Frequently our teacher digressed, nowadays. Geography centred around the Western Front. We were entertained with stories of our soldiers' and allies' bravery. Tales of enemy atrocities were substantiated by the appearance of Belgian families who came to live in the district.

Opportunities to 'wag it' from school increased. One could excuse one's absence by lies of being detained in food queues.

But birthdays were shattering old associations. Billy, the 'cock o' the school', being fatherless, applied for his release on his thirteenth birthday. He had work promised in an engineering shop. One by one the old faces disappeared.

My own birthday was fast approaching. I looked forward to it with much excitement. I wanted the freedom of a full-time job; my evenings free and lots of money in my pocket. Everything was in the future.

Seventeen years ago, a few days after my thirteenth birthday, the headmaster gave me a testimonial and shook hands with me. I ran out into the schoolyard yelling with triumph. My schooldays were over and I was free to find a full-time job.

I was envied.

THE CONFORMER

[Harrow]

BY L. P. HARTLEY

RUMBLING along between Rome and Venice, sleepless in a so-called sleeping-car, I reviewed my time at Harrow, urging my memories to assume the ironical character suggested by the title of this book. Insomnia induces vindictiveness: I shall have no difficulty, I thought, in finding grievances. First of all the insomnia itself. The chief thing that was keeping me awake was the fear that when we reached Venice I should be sound asleep and so be carried on to Trieste. Not a very rational fear, for the conductor was sure to rouse me, but my mind could not rest, and why? Because for five years I had lived in continual dread of being late for First School. It had left a dent on my consciousness, inflicted a Freudian bruise from which I should never recover. 'Bell on!' How well I remembered that menacing phrase. It meant gulping down one's cocoa and burning one's mouth and choking over one's biscuit, ruinous for the digestion; or in extreme cases, starting out without any food at all, thereby stunting one's growth and sowing the seeds of lifelong malnutrition. And the only result of this enforced punctuality was, that I had never been able to be in time for any appointment since. Reacting

65

against tyranny and the punishments with which it was enforced, I had found the idea of punctuality odious, a mark of servitude whose every association was distasteful.

Insomnia, nervous apprehension, indigestion, mal-nutrition, arrested growth, an ingrained habit of un-punctuality: all these crippling disabilities could be laid at the door of my old school. 'What matter, I learnt them at Harrow!' I thought bitterly, consulting my watch and finding it was half-past six. But presently I began to consider my grievances *seriatim*. Insomnia: I had suffered from it before I went to Harrow, and after; but during my time there I could not recollect one sleepless night. Then as to nervous apprehension, it was certain that of late years I had grown increasingly timid: I was afraid of thunder-storms, of meeting cows in the road, of driving a motor car. When I scratched myself I envisaged the possi-bility of lockjaw, and I never had a cold that I did not think would turn to pneumonia. The idea of saying a few words in public disturbed me for days. But when I was at Harrow, I remembered, these things afflicted me much less. I played football in the rain without ever expecting trouble to come of it. Once when I was knocked down (the Harrow game can be fairly rough, as anyone who has played it will testify) I bit the end of my tongue and had two stitches put in it: but I was not at all dismayed; I felt a hero and even got one or two friends to treat me as such. As to illness, in those days I rather welcomed it than otherwise; to 'stop out', with 'no admittance' pinned

66

to my door, made an agreeable change from the routine of school life. I listened with satisfaction to the patter of footsteps scurrying off to school, and recked nothing of a rising temperature. Indeed, I sometimes wished these visitations would come oftener and were less easily kept at bay by the salubrious air of Harrow Hill. I suffered, no doubt, even then from the fear of coming events, but not too severely, and I could carry off with a high hand situations which would appal me now. As Head of the House I did not shrink from summoning my subjects to my room, telling them how awful they were and what a thankless and distasteful job it was to have their welfare in my charge; nor did I mind 'whopping' delinquents and I occasionally took practice shots against the curtain of my bed to get my hand in. Whereas now, unless I lose my temper, I cannot bring myself to utter a rebuke, however well merited. *Quantum mutatus ab illo* . . . As to malnutrition, I was certainly thinner then than I am now. But my present state is one that I am always bewailing and it would be captious to complain, in retrospect, of a figure to whose meagreness, or something approaching it, I should be now only too delighted to attain.

The more I thought about it, the more I realized that the objections to the Public School system which I have often voiced, and with the greatest conviction, were not founded on my own experience at Harrow. At least most of them were not. For instance, the familiar charge that public schools turn out all boys according to a pattern, did not hold good of my contemporaries at Harrow. Certainly in my own house the boys were as unlike each other as they could well be; and whatever personal peculiarities, pleasant or unpleasant, they started with, time and the influence of the school only seemed to foster. Looking back I see that we were a collection of oddities such as would have rejoiced the heart of Herbert Spencer or any individualist philosopher. We were split up into small groups, one or two in competition with each other but the rest practically self-sufficing.

Of course these divisions ceased to operate in matters that concerned the house as a whole. In games and all the activities in which we were in competition with other houses the 'team spirit' infected every one; and though occasionally the Head of the House or the Captain of Football would foment it artificially with alarming minatory harangues, threatening lack of keenness with the direst penalties, I for one never found much difficulty in feeling or exhibiting the necessary enthusiasm. Except in matters connected with the Corps. The Corps never had any glamour for me, and on field-days I used to attend the rather inglorious 'non-corps schools', with hardly a twinge of humiliation. Nor, in war-time when the corps became compulsory, did I feel I had missed anything; section-rushes among the bracken at Beaconsfield or Berkhamsted gave me little pleasure. But in the early days no pressure was brought upon one, at any rate in my house, to join the Corps.

With football it was different. Football could only be avoided with the help of a medical certificate. I must confess that I never really enjoyed football. Most of the few unpleasant memories I have of Harrow are connected with it. I always had a lurking fear, not of the game, but of making a fool of myself. By running about industriously among the forwards one could reduce the chances of this to a minimum. Those dread words, 'Hartley, you must buck up and do something' were seldom addressed to me. But try as one would to escape notice and lie hid (the irregular and equivocal verb λανθάνω might have been invented to describe my demeanour on the football field), there always came a moment when one's maladroitness was shown up. One failed to give the Captain an easy 'yards'. That was the worst thing that could happen — worse than failing, oneself, to score a base off 'yards'; for then one had at any rate the glory of the attempt, whereas to deprive a 'fez' of the chance to distinguish himself was a disaster that had nothing to mitigate it. Strangely enough, owing to the intrigues of the higher powers and through no merit of my own, I eventually became captain of the house team, several players of superior capacity being passed over in my favour. It was a difficult position, nominally of great dignity but full of secret mortification. In House Games my side invariably lost unless I fortified it with all the strongest players — a desperate remedy, which I adopted more often than was really decent. The alternative was not to have any House Games and, as this lay within the discretion of the captain, they were as infrequent as possible during my term of office.

School boys are an extremely reticent race. I do

not know how much my contemporaries enjoyed House Games, or whether, like me, they narrowly studied the captain at dinner as he sat with paper and pencil before him, deciding our fate. If he wrinkled his brow and consulted his august neighbours and wrote a lot, it meant a House Game; if he ignored the envelope and merely scribbled something on it at the end of the meal, the situation was saved: we should have 'Ex for All'.

'Ex for All' was an institution of divine origin. It meant that we had the afternoon free, with no obligation except to change and clear out of the house until it was time for Bill. Failure to comply with this regulation was punishable, like many other offences, with a 'whopping', but I do not remember anyone ever being whopped for it. Indeed, the temptation to stay in was of the slightest; there were so many attractions outside: fives and squash, kicking a 'fug' about in the 'plains below' (I never understood why I enjoyed this form of football so much and disliked the regular kind: I suppose it was the absence of supervision and of the fear of being 'cursed'); or one could take a 'run' with a friend in one's own time and at one's own pace, combining exercise with conversation. There was a kind of tradition that one should come back muddy and sweat-stained, and if a 'fez' saw one slink in spick-and-span and unruffled he might give one a black look or a word of caution, usually phrased in the most wounding terms; but nothing else happened. I still remember the delicious sense of freedom that pervaded those afternoons. They represented our life at its most care-free and relaxed: we were responsible to no one but ourselves. Whereas when 'footer' was the order of the day — 'Harrow footer on Harrow clay' — it was all tension and effort and keeping oneself up to scratch: life at its most strenuous, with failure and humiliation and even corporal punishment always in the offing.

The summer term was dominated by cricket, and cricket, as every schoolboy knows, is a much less serious affair than football; consequently the summer term had a halcyon air. At football it is the inexpert who suffer. They feel, and are encouraged to feel, their worthlessness, their slackness, their clumsiness, they are told that they are, from every point of view, superfluous, a disgrace to the House. With cricket the case is altered. In cricket it is the good players who suffer; they are constantly losing their form, they come with a great reputation from their private schools and fail to justify it; they have runs of bad luck; they sink from one eleven to another; they are given extra fielding practice; they spend tedious hours at the nets; they fail to get their caps, or, if they get them, cease from that moment to make runs or take wickets. They have little to win and much to lose. They live in an atmosphere of uncertain glory, like an April day, balanced between dizzy success and dismal failure: a nerve-racking position. Whereas the mediocre performers, of whom I was one, have a much better time. They belong to some low-grade, ironically-named side, 'Nondescripts' or 'Professors'; nothing is expected of them, and if by a happy chance they do distinguish themselves, they are praised beyond their deserts. Cricket was a game that could be played on two planes of reality: first on the pitch itself, indifferently, and secondly in imagination, or in the person of a chosen hero, magnificently. No game lent itself to the imagination as did cricket; one might enjoy it more, played vicariously, than at the wicket. The match at Lord's was the apotheosis, the supreme rite of the cricket cult; then one identified oneself with every member of the side, suffered in their failures, exulted in their triumphs. The Summer Term was a romantic term and, if it never quite attained the lyrical ecstasy expressed in 'Ducker' (in my time one of the most popular of School songs) it imprinted itself on the memory as a recurrent Golden Age when the lion of Authority lay down with its subject lambs, and the harsher aspects of reality were veiled. The gradual recession of lock-up till it reached eight o'clock, increased one's sense of freedom; the two perfect hours after Six Bill enfolded a leisure so perfect one could almost apprehend it physically, like a caress.

In the Michaelmas Term life became real and earnest again. In the Michaelmas Term Harrow approximated most nearly to what people mean by a Public School when they use the words as a term of reproach. (The Easter Term, as is well known lacks character: it is provisional and experimental; it is shorter than the others; it is full of false starts and impotent conclusions; it has no settled rhythm; illness plays a considerable part in it, at least it did in my time.) In the Summer Term we were in a sense spectators; we delegated our individual responsibilities to the School Eleven, which represented us at the great pageant of Lord's. If we were not ourselves encouraged to criticize our betters, we were comparatively free from their criticism. But in the Michaelmas Term we were actors whose performance was jealously watched. We had to render an account of ourselves. We had to toe the line. Gone was the fantasy of summer, the *saturnia regna* so happily expressed in 'Willow the King' and 'Ducker'. Our winter outlook was summed up in songs of sterner import: 'Tom', 'Yards', 'October', songs that celebrated the ardours and endurances of the football field.

> October brings the cold weather in
> When the winds and the rains continue;
> He urges the limbs that have lazy grown
> And braces the languid sinew.

The main pressure of discipline came not from the masters nor from our contemporaries but from older boys. The sixth-formers wielded it in virtue of their office, but others, 'caps', 'fezzes', 'four-yearers' and 'three-yearers' exerted, or could exert if they chose, an influence almost equally great. As I said, one's contemporaries tended to leave one alone. I well remember my first evening at Harrow; how I sat apprehensively in my small room, comforting myself with a handbook to Lincoln Cathedral and expecting every moment that hostile hordes would pour in, ask me a number of painful and impertinent questions, and trample the precious volume under foot. Nothing of the sort happened; no one paid me the slightest attention; I even began to feel a trifle lonely. Nor was I ever 'ragged' in the House, in spite of being what was known as a 'groize', i.e. someone who worked harder than was necessary or desirable. Once, I remember, when I was in a very low form some overgrown youths who still lingered in it (superannuation was not enforced in those days as it is now) amused themselves by throwing snowballs at me; but either their malice melted with the melting of the snow, or they were too lazy or unimaginative to invent new annoyances: anyhow their unwelcome attentions ceased.

Speaking for my own House I must say that personal eccentricity, though often remarked upon, was treated with the utmost tolerance. As long as you did not offend against some code, you were allowed to go your own way. Transgression against tradition was a very serious matter, though the severity of the punishments varied enormously, being determined by the reigning Head of the House, and the Captains of cricket and football and those whom they delighted to honour. My house had a tendency to decentralization which, from the point of view of success at games, was a drawback, but I cannot help thinking that our private lives were much happier for it. I remember one term when all the several powers suddenly saw eye to eye, and a very uncomfortable term it was. They decided that the House needed 'waking up'; hardly an evening passed without a 'whopping', the sinister sounds echoing down the corridor from the Head of the House's room. In their reforming zeal the Sixth-formers snatched at any straw. A friend of mine and I were 'whopped' for being late for House-singing. I protested to the Head of the House that I had been in time by my watch, which was right by the School clock. 'Ah,' said he with a fearful smile, 'but here we go by the *House* time.' My friend explained (so he assured me afterwards) that according to the House clock he had not been late — only to be told with (I suppose) the same grim inflexion, 'Ah, but here we go by the *School* time.' On one occasion the whole House was summarily dealt with. Some wag had decorated the lower regions with festoons of paper; the effect had a certain gaiety, though the uniformity of colour in the streamers was monotonous. The culprit refused to come forward and we were all made to suffer. When my turn came the executioners, attired in running vests, were bright-eyed, sweating and exultant, but seemed rather tired. It turned out they were not.

This mild epidemic of flagellation subsided as suddenly as it broke out, and having (I suppose) achieved its object, was never repeated. Nominally, one could suffer corporal punishment for a multitude of misdemeanours: leaning too far out of the window on Sunday, letting a Sixth-former's fire out when 'on boy', walking in the middle of the High Street when not a 'blood' or in the company of a 'blood'. Every year the new Head of the House posted up a list of Three- and Four-year Privileges (in the main regulations regarding dress), infringement of which was punishable by 'whopping'; but I do not remember a case of a non-three-yearer being chastised for wearing coloured socks or a grey flannel waistcoat or a barmaid-collar, or for having his 'bluer' turned up at the neck.

Looking back one may think this careful tabulation of taboos slightly ridiculous and marvel at the awe in which we held them. But the sumptuary laws did serve a purpose — it would have been impracticable to let every boy wear what he liked — and, moreover, they cleared up the whole question of 'putting on side'. To invent a kind of Eighteenth Amendment or Volstead Act forbidding schoolboys to 'swank' is clearly doomed to failure. Some form of personal boastfulness is inherent in schoolboy nature; it cannot be eradicated; but at Harrow it is at any rate canalized and charted. We could not prevent people betraying by their looks and gestures that they had an overweening opinion of themselves; but we did contrive that, unless entitled by seniority, they should be denied the grosser forms of self-assertion. The privilege system was in a sense a democratic ordinance, for it allowed a share of self-glory to the humble and obscure, who would never have attained it by the unaided lustre of their own personalities. Thus they enjoyed a kind of old-age pension paid not in coin but (commodities much dearer to the schoolboy heart) in dignity and influence and prestige.

The question of personal ascendency and how it is to be regulated is a vital problem in institutions like public schools, where the boys not only work and play but live together. School life is a microcosm in which operate, unconsciously but intensely, most of the instincts and passions that agitate the outside world.

The majority of boys are avid of success, and the glory accruing therefrom; but the struggle to rise above the ruck is fiercer than it is in later life, because in nearly all cases it depends on some quality of personality which the rest are forced or charmed into recognizing. Rank or wealth was not enough to secure it; we were almost indifferent as to whose father was rich, or whose had a title. Proficiency at games did not ensure it, neither did scholarship debar from it. By being beautiful, by being wicked, by being a wit, by being a butt, by being good-natured, by being foul-mouthed (a field, however, in which pre-eminence was hard to win), by being daring, by being always in trouble, one could attain a certain measure of popularity; but one might be any of these things, one might be that phoenix, the 'good all-round boy' of the song, and remain a nonentity. Public opinion was extraordinarily sensitive as to whose star was rising and whose setting. It is hardly fanciful to say that every member of the House, except the Olympians at the top, had a pretty shrewd idea not only of how each boy counted with his fellows, but also of where he stood in his own esteem.

Vanity of vanities . . . but it was this very insecurity which made school life so exciting. Every week some valley was exalted, some mountain or hill laid low. Whether this wear and tear of the emotions is a good thing, I cannot say. It certainly leads in some cases to emotional atrophy. The necessity of disguising what one felt, of keeping the famous stiff upper lip when cursed by a Sixth-former, or wounded by a friend, or hit by a cricket ball, sometimes found its logical outcome: after many repetitions one felt nothing at all. 'Afflictions induce callosities', said Sir Thomas Browne. The phlegmatic Englishman is often phlegmatic because he has lost the power of expressing emotion. He has repressed his feelings so often that there are none left to repress. But I do not remember any cases of inward mortification at Harrow. We had a great deal of freedom and a great deal of leisure; old friendships broke up or wore out, but others took their place. One generally had something to look forward to. One's state and one's status altered with every term and it needed no great effort of imagination to persuade oneself that they had altered for the better.

I was too unsophisticated, as I think most of us were, to isolate myself mentally from the complex of taboos and obligations which comprised our life, and find their symbolism hollow. Almost to the last it seemed glorious, the worthy goal of a life's endeavour, to wear a bow-tie and a braided waistcoat and write letters on the notepaper of the Philathletic Club. If I was praised I glowed; if I was reproved I trembled. I accepted praise and censure uncritically. I had musical pretensions but I thought the Harrow Songs beautiful, and if I could not always enter into their sentiment, I felt it was my fault. I lived too much in the moment to nourish wistful feelings about the spire of Harrow Church, or the elms of the Sixth-form ground, but I envied those who did. I had a great respect for Authority and trembled at its nod; I did not much enjoy exercising it, but that, I afterwards discovered, was a temperamental defect. I was transported with delight if asked out to dinner by the Head-master or W.G.Y. or C.W.M.M., and I should be still. In all my life I can remember no sensations more deliriously exciting than seeing Blount and Wilson make their centuries at Lord's. In fact there were few occasions when the School piped and I did not dance, or mourned and I did not lament. And I think it was the same with most of us. We found it easy to accept the School's standards: we responded to its lures; we cut our coats figuratively as well as literally according to the cloth it supplied. No doubt there were some boys who lived in a world of the imagination to which Harrow contributed only the setting. I had friends who treated the school as a kind of hotel, useful as providing a night's lodging, but quite inadequate as a stage for the drama of their lives. Sturdy natures succeeded in thus keeping the school at arm's length, paying tribute, as it were, while they conducted the real business of existence in regions, imaginative or actual, into which it did not intrude. Others, less hardy, tried and failed. They were generally unhappy and should have been taken away. But in most of us the instinct towards conformity was strong enough to assimilate unpalatable experience, or reject it without too much disturbance of the nervous centres.

I was law-abiding and industrious and so I missed the important and exciting side of school life which consists in being at odds with authority. Approval was what I sought, and I was only too eager (unlike some of my contemporaries) to accept it from all and sundry. I had neither the spirit nor the inclination to 'rag' the masters; when others did it I joined nervously in the general laugh, but I was never a ringleader, even in such minor escapades as blocking up the form-room keyhole with paper, or writing out French 'rep' on the master's own blackboard. I deplore this timidity, but I am glad I did not try to overcome it, for the role of revolutionary would not have suited me and I profited more by sitting receptive at the feet of my pastors and masters than I should have done by buzzing, mosquito-like, about their ears. If they despised me for this attitude they were, on the whole, magnanimous enough not to show it. Thus, though I never won the plaudits of my fellows for (say) powdering my form-master's neck with a substance called Russian Flea, I escaped the counter-attacks for which some of the staff were justly famous. My first form-master did not seize me by the short hair above the ears, or make me sit on a form alone, with the flex of the reading-lamp twisted lightly round my neck, a painless but humiliating position, nor did he ever say to me, 'Whatever you look like, boy, don't look like Mrs. . . .' (naming the wife of one of his colleagues). In V¹ I kept careful watch over my vocabulary, and managed to avoid the phrase 'stir up' (almost inevitable in construing many Latin authors) and the thunderous exclamation 'Porridge!' with which E. G. always greeted it. Nor had he occasion to address to me the famous harangue beginning, 'Boy, you have said what you know to be wrong, next you'll do what you know to be wrong, then . . .' and so on through a series of ever blacker crimes, culminating in the murder of one's grandmother and death by hanging. The form-master of the Lower Sixth was a man with an extremely fine mind, an impressive presence, a wonderful command of English, and a tongue that was justly dreaded. He was formidable even in his lighter moments. As he passed one's desk he would say: 'If you put your hat there I shall tread on it, and I weigh fourteen stone.' When one made a blunder he forbore for a moment from comment; perhaps he was thinking it out, for it was generally devastating when it came. But in more genial moods he would remark, 'If you ever say that again I shall fall on you with my teeth and my umbrella'; or, with a slightly hissing intake of breath, 'May I appeal to Heaven to strike me pink.'

The most irrepressible among my contemporaries held him in awe. Nor was G.T.W. to be trifled with; he was man of moods, and one could not always please him simply by trying to. But he was a teacher of the first order and he got more out of his pupils than it seemed in their power to give. He was a genius. The Staff did not hold many like him, but I do not remember being up to a master who did not in a greater or less degree attempt to understand as well as teach one. The gift of appreciation is rare and it is surprising that so many schoolmasters should still have it, after all they have gone through. I never found it lacking among the 'beeks' at Harrow. The lessons in self-knowledge gained from one's school-fellows were seldom gently administered and seldom calculated to increase self-confidence. The masters almost always displayed a strong sense of responsibility in the bestowal of praise and blame. Both my house-masters had a remarkable gift for entering into one's life and clarifying its problems; they could not have been more helpful had they been bound by firmer ties than the supposedly flimsy one of pedagogue and pupil. And so it was with the rest: they took infinite pains to discover a lurking aptitude and bring it into the daylight. So far from ignoring or snubbing potential ability, they often created it out of material which seemed as unpromising to its owner as to everyone else. Of course they could not work miracles, and they often encountered a stubborn resistance to the sweet influences of education comparable to that of the badger in its hole. But try they did. Gardening has been called the purest of human pleasures; there is certainly no action more beautiful and disinterested than the attempt to give the human plant the care and encouragement best suited to its case. Such solicitude was always forthcoming in my time at Harrow, if one cared to avail oneself of it. The influence exerted by the school as a whole was so general and far-reaching that one cannot estimate it any more than one can calculate the effect of being born of different parents or in another country. But the peculiar mental stimulus derived from, say, E.C.E.O., G.T.W., P.C.B. or C.W.M.M. (some of them had nicknames, but too irreverent and misleading for quotation) was as definite and recognizable as the course of a river on a map. I shall always be grateful for their inspiration and regret that it was not more lasting.

PITY THE PEDAGOGUE

[Wellington]

BY HAROLD NICOLSON

I HAVE been reading recently Alain's *Propos sur l'Education*, a work in which that precise Norman — (confident, as always, in the validity of his personal experience, as in his own habits of correct discussion) — proclaims his opposition to the psychological treatment of the young. With shrewd precision he joins issue with the whole school of tender educationalists, from Montessori to Jung, from Dalton to Dartington Hall.

Alain possesses an almost Socratic talent for reducing to their most humiliating terms those problems which we are ourselves apt to modify by clothing thought in sentiment, fact in desires. To Alain's mind the psychological pedagogue is unaware of the true purpose of all early education, which is not so much to force intelligence, or to inculcate knowledge, as to foster will. He has no sympathy for those who would teach the child only what he enjoys, even as he has nothing but pity for those schoolmasters who endeavour personally to understand their pupils before they confer upon them the rhythm of impersonal discipline. In Alain's opinion 'the interesting is always uninstructive'; 'il faut savoir', he writes, 's'ennuyer d'abord'. The actual effort of learning appears to him more important even than the thing learnt, 'la difficulté vaincue' more valuable than any temporary interest that may be aroused; 'above all,' he says, 'let us have no sugar'. He observes, and rightly, that the mentality of the child is in process of constant mutation and that what seemed interesting to the boy in February will by June appear, not dull merely, but a trifle shaming. There is a danger even that some of this retrospective contempt (felt by every intelligent schoolboy for what he learnt easily some months ago) may be transferred to the teacher who provided him with this, at the time, pleasurable stimulus. Conversely, the habit of rhythmic obedience, 'la difficulté vaincue', leads to no such reactions. It furnishes continuous embankments between which the waters of infant intelligence can sparkle happily, and withal respectfully, upon their way. The Montessori mother, in Alain's eyes, is merely digging holes in the bank. For him the ideal schoolmaster should avoid all individual analysis and should be impersonal to the point of heartlessness. It should be left to the father and mother to apply those psychological unguents which the more sensitive child may require: a school must be 'something different': its main social function is to awake the individual from the bio-logical slumber of the family; its main personal func-tion is the creation of will. In the exercise of these functions a school must be something rigid, impersonal, just, combative and cold.

It pleases me to find one of the more objective of modern French thinkers thus justifying in almost philosophical terms that hazy tendency towards disciplinarian education which we call the public school system. For those who look back upon their own schooldays with horror but respect it is satisfactory to be provided by a foreign intellectual with a logical formula such as excuses our horror while explaining, and thereby justifying, our respect. And it is a relief to be furnished with a perfectly firm basis for defending not merely the superb luxuries of a classical curriculum, but also the crudities of a system aimed primarily at the formation of what we call 'character' and of what Alain, with some difference of meaning, describes as 'will'.

Our own schoolmasters to-day would seem to have lost the courage of their former convictions. We find Mr. Roxborough flirting crossly with the defeatists, and even to the firm features of Dr. Norwood is affixed at moments the ingratiating smile of Montessori motherhood. Yet the day may be approaching when the enlightened schoolmaster will concentrate his progressiveness upon hygiene (a most belated concentration) and will, in his strictly pedagogic theory, become once again magnificently unreasonable, nobly out of date. It must be admitted, of course, that within the last generation three events have occurred which will render difficult any return to the old line of entrenchments. The public school of the pre-war period was designed to provide a large number of standardized young men fitted for the conquest, administration and retention of a vast Oriental Empire. There are now no more areas to be conquered; the opportunities for administration will be increasingly restricted; and the prospects of retention, momentarily at least, seem insecure. Concurrently the decline both in unearned income and in employment has induced in parents a mood of perhaps unthinking panic and an illusion that a 'practical' or 'modern' education may prove more materially profitable than would eight years spent upon the humanities. And in the third place the emancipation of women has done much to render acute the eternal mother problem and to induce in the mothers of England an inconveniently combative disbelief in this man-made system, a desire to criticize those virile traditions which in pre-war days were accepted as inevitable. No wonder that our pedagogues should bury the patri-archal past in regretful silence and endeavour to placate the matriarchal future with voluble but variable babblings of conciliation.

Yet need they feel so ashamed? Alain will tell them that the old theory can be justified in modern terms and that the new theory is all too often but an escape from topical fact. True it is that, whereas the enemies of the old system are active, educated, articulate and convinced; its defenders are uncertain, illiterate and often incapable of framing their emotions in shapes of thought or even language. Our public schools have thus suffered, not so much from the skill of their opponents, as from the ineptitude of their allies: it is very difficult to save the old system from its friends. How unfortunate is it, for instance, that the most ardent supporters of the old system should be those

old boys who have *not* done very well in after life.
How regrettable that to the more occupied or successful man, his school days have receded into a haze,
suffused sometimes with the pink colouring of sentimental youth — but concealing more often the
period of greatest boredom in his own biography — a
period of which he thinks vaguely, distastefully, or not
at all. A public school is thus apt to be justified only
by those of its children who have failed to express their
personalities in any other walk of life; nor are such the
children by or of whom one would wish to be either
protected or acclaimed.

My heart, for such reasons, throbs with pity for the
schoolmaster.   Consider the eternal falsity of his position; those successive insincerities in which, owing to
his profession, he is obliged to indulge. Upon the face
and fabric of an adult schoolmaster these alternations
of attitude have left their cruel mark. Authority mani-
fests itself, not in the secure gestures of proconsular or
ministerial dignity, but in a look at once costive, fleet-
ing and sly; a look induced by constant preoccupation
with the surface of that dignity rather than with its
foundations. Every schoolmaster, after the age of
forty-nine, is inclined to flatulence, is apt to swallow
frequently and to puff. Observe, also, the self-consciousness with which, when away from the school
buildings, the schoolmaster mingles with the outer
world. No dentist could be more self-protective, more
apologetic, more almost repudiatory, about his own
profession. Well he knows that the whole human race
is divided between those who are, or will be parents,

and those who are, or have been, boys. Well he knows that it is not for him to mingle with his fellows in terms of natural human companionship. Clumsily does he flop (poor ungainly polygon) from that facet of obsequious affability to that facet of a dignity the proportions of which are unjustified by personal achievement — resting at moments upon that third safe and withal cordial plane of test-match heartiness, discussing the immediately uninteresting in a voice a little louder than is necessary, or agreeable, or even fair. Poor man — the virtues which he possesses are not ostensible — seldom is it accorded to any human to discourse at length upon the iambic trimeter in a London club. Suspicious is he also of those who, however tactfully, display an interest in the more recent problems of his calling. Is this a young parent taking soundings? Is this an old boy meditating revenge? Inevitably does the schoolmaster retreat from these alternatives behind the quadruple barriers of flatulence, affability, good taste, and bowling averages.

Yet Alain tells us that the ideal schoolmaster should be heroic, heartless, impersonal and just. Alain is discussing mainly the French primary school. Yet I pause at his remark. I question my own experience. Having since many years emerged from the school age I can survey the problem with an impartiality uncoloured, I hope, by any desire to see the younger generation suffer those inhumanities which I myself endured. Do I agree with Alain? Did I, in other words, benefit more from the personal or the impersonal type of schoolmaster? Through whom, and in what manner, did I myself derive profit from my school-days? To what defects in the system, or in myself, do I attribute the strange fact that it took me so many years to recover from the shock of school? It seems to me to-day that I owe everything in life first to my parents and secondly to Balliol; and that my debt to my private and my public school is far outweighed by the claims they made upon my courage and individuality. Is this a just accusation? I do not think that it is wholly just. I can make it only subject to certain reservations.

One forgets, in the first place, that those eight years were years of continuous change. From the age of nine to thirteen one was still in the phase of biological somnolence. From the age of thirteen to sixteen the battle was joined, and actually won, between individuality and environment. And if, on emerging from puberty, life suddenly became a matter of personal enjoyment, this revelation cannot always be attributed to the brilliance and sympathy of one's own post-puberty masters, or the previous years of darkness be ascribed to the inhumanity of those who, in patient endurance, coped with the sombre obstinacies of the chrysalis stage.

In the second place, a man of adult years is apt to forget that such wisdom as he believes himself to have acquired is based upon habits of behaviour, grooves of memory, which were induced and drilled during the unconscious stage of his development and without which his more conscious development would have lacked either root or foundation. We are always apt to ascribe our own processes of enlightenment to positive influences which can be remembered and even quoted, rather than to those negative influences which, because they were unpleasant, are buried deep in the vaults of the unconscious. We are thus, in our vanity, grateful for recollected encouragement; we are not in the least grateful for forgotten, although perhaps more valuable, snubs. And, when I think of all this, my heart again goes out in sympathy to those whose business it is to impose habits of conduct upon pre-puberty boys. Their life is one long series of betrayals. It is among thistles that they sow their seed.

I am conscious, moreover (even at moments of intense vituperation) of a marked distaste for those who have not benefited by a public school education. This distaste is based on no superficial prejudice; it is founded on experience. People who have not endured the restrictive shaping of an English school are apt in after life to be ego-centric, formless and inconsiderate. These are irritating faults. They are inclined, also, to show off. This objectionable brand of vanity is in its turn destructive of the more creative forms of intelligence. Surely I am unfitted to condemn, or even to criticize, a system, the absence of which induces in me movements of such continued distaste?

And yet, and yet . . .

Take, for instance, the question of encouragement. agree with Alain that the sugared type of pedagogy is a mistake and I admit that I myself benefited enormously by the snubs that I received. Yet need they have been so arbitrary, so fortuitous and so explicit? On the whole I was good at work; on the whole

I was very bad at games. Yet I am not conscious that at any moment during the first seven years of my education it was ever suggested to me that I might, by scholarship, counterbalance the disgrace which was deservedly and unfalteringly mine in the region of athletics. I am certain, for instance, that had I displayed with ball or bat the same promise as I displayed in Greek iambics, I should have been made to feel that with care and application some sort of future opened before me. Until my last year at Wellington no such suggestion was ever made, and I seriously believe that this omission retarded the growth of any self-confidence or 'will' or even 'character' for seven shrouded years.

I am thus convinced that, in my own case, a little more intellectual encouragement would have done me not harm, but good. I do not think I am exaggerating when I say that we boys derived the impression at Wellington that intellectual prowess was in some way effeminate, and that it was only by physical prowess that one could manifest, or even subscribe to, that aim of 'manliness' for which alone we had all, teleologically, been sent to Berkshire. My diffidence, my self-distrust, may, it is true, have produced an irritating bounciness of manner which my masters and fellows rightly considered should be suppressed. But I cannot convince myself that a more intelligent pedagogue should not have observed that I was seriously anxious to *learn;* or that it would have been impossible for him, with a little firm handling, to have suppressed the bounciness without destroying the bounce.

As it was, both were deflated; for years my whole conscious energy was concentrated upon the necessity of seeming manly, of giving no offence. Those years were, if not wasted, then absorbed by energies which ought to have been supplementary only, but which became central. Nor was it merely that I was denied in my studies that encouragement which I should certainly have received had I shown an equal capacity for games. It was that I was exposed to definite discouragement. Two instances of such discouragement have remained for ever imprinted on my mind.

The first incident arose in connection with the funeral oration of Pericles. I must have been almost sixteen at the time and I remember that it was the end of the Easter term. The almond tree against the pink brick of the laboratory building showed a dissonance of colour and the lilac buds which for many months had appeared green and promising were beginning to darken and expand. I had been immured in the Sanatorium recovering from chicken-pox and while I was still convalescent but infectious I was given the funeral speech to translate into the English tongue. Some coincidence between the re-birth of the year and the re-birth of my own energies induced in me what might be called a tremulous frame of mind, or in any case a frame of mind susceptible to fresh emotions. In so far as I can be certain of anything, I am certain that this was the first occasion upon which the Greek language appeared to me as something more than a daily difficulty to be conquered, as possessing a vitality, and even a beauty, of its own. The speech struck me, and still strikes me, as one of the finest pieces of human prose. And thus, having completed my translation with the aid of the lexicon I did what I had never done before — I endeavoured to render into English some of the high resonance which, even at that date, I had detected in the original. I am prepared to believe that my translation, when completed and so patiently revised, was a bombastic effort. I suppose that my form-master imagined that, even if I had done the thing myself, I was obviously showing off. 'We worship beauty', I had written, 'with a consciousness of its purpose, we philosophize without softness.' Not perhaps a very good translation, but one which should have indicated at least that I had been interested and taken pains. In after years it has struck me that this famous apophthegm must in itself have been disturbing to the average schoolmaster. It comes in the middle of a rhetorical idealization of all those qualities which are supposed (quite wrongly) to forge a link between all that was best in the Greek spirit and all that was best in the spirit of our public schools. Yet this phrase, if rightly considered, cuts across so comforting an analogy. To the average schoolmaster aesthetics can serve no purpose, whether good or bad. To the average schoolmaster the love of knowledge can scarcely be associated with any softness. I have since reflected that it must be galling to the schoolmaster that Pericles should have chosen to shape his sentence exactly that way round. Had he spoken of the dangers of softness which lurk in any aestheticism there would have been much doctrine and much comfort to be derived. Had he spoken of the teleological importance of learning, here again he would have been showing agreement with everything that, at Wellington College, was taught in 1904. Unfortunately he spoke of the function of aesthetics and the menaces of learning. I do not wonder that in stressing the dangerous implications which the words contained I was regarded by my master as displaying not bumptiousness only but bad taste. Yet it would have been so easy for him to have told me that I had translated that particular passage both inaccurately and in false English. He failed to adopt this sympathetic course: hence my grievance.

Had he delivered such a rebuke, my grievance would not, after so many years, have remained so vivid to me. He delivered no such frontal attack: he approached me (as I still think, meanly) upon the flank. 'The worst,' he said, 'about asking boys to do some work at the Sanatorium is that they always get some older boy to do the work for them. I congratulate you, Nicolson, upon your skill in this respect.'

To this day, I gnash my teeth at the ineptitude of this remark. Its results were inevitable. I now see of course that the only way in which I could have diminished this impression of dishonesty would have been to raise all my other work from that moment to the same elevated and pretentious standard. Even had I realized this necessity, I should not have had the time. That translation had taken me four long days. Never again would I be able to expend so much time upon a single piece of work. I concluded, therefore, that if I were to avoid the charge of cribbing, I must always do my work slightly below my own level. And many months were wasted in this diminution.

Many years afterwards I met in London the very master who had imposed upon me this injustice. I told him the story. He was immensely amused. 'Well,' he said, 'I *do* call that bad luck! I don't wonder that you felt annoyed. But if I remember rightly you were a conceited boy at the time and I expect it did you a world of good.' Conceited? — I was tortured by diffidence. A world of good? — that single incident obstructed my education for seven long months; after which (for I was fortunate) I emerged into the sixth form and entered the exciting, and withal placid, and above all Aegean atmosphere of Dr. Pollock's tutelage.

The second incident was equally deplorable and also rankles to this day. We were not taught English at Wellington but on one occasion in the Lower Sixth we were asked, for some odd reason, to write an essay. In so far as I remember it was the only essay which at Wellington I was ever asked to write. The subject chosen was 'Essay upon a piece of coal'. I presumed that what was required was not so much a discourse upon the Industrial Revolution as an examination of the responses and associations evoked by the contemplation of coal in detail. I took much trouble about that essay; the result, I am sure, was ridiculous in the extreme. Yet I have a feeling that my own essay, turgid and pretentious though it must have been, should have indicated that here was a person anxious to experiment, if not in ideas, then at least in the handling of words. I am pretty sure of this, since when, but twelve months later, I went to Balliol my essays were not wholly disregarded. Yet when the unhappy and expected day arrived when our essays were returned, our form-master announced that Maclaren's essay was the best and that mine was by far the worst. 'In order,' he said, 'to show you how *not* to write an essay I shall now read you some passages from Nicolson's production.' He did so. The merriment displayed by my school-fellows was, under such deliberate provocation, unbounded. I suffered more acutely than I have suffered intellectually either before or since. And on returning to my house afterwards in the unwelcome company of the triumphant Maclaren he broke the grim silence which marked our footsteps with what, I now realize, were meant to be words of comfort. 'Yes,' he said, 'I always thought that you were a little mad.'

Alain, I suppose, would contend that such humiliations are good for one. I think that the effect would have been less damaging had the rebuke been administered with less overt cruelty and had there been occasion to repair my disgrace. The cruelty was blatant: no other occasion arose. And the result was that my buds of literary interest were nipped by this inclement frost.

I recognize to-day that this was perhaps an excellent thing. Had the master in question decided that this public humiliation, by retarding premature exuberance, would in the end be valuable, I should feel for him to-day nothing but the deepest gratitude. I know however that he came to no such decision. He observed only that my own essay was 'different' from those of the other boys and concluded, either that I had taken no trouble, or that I was endeavouring to show off. These were incorrect conclusions. They would not have been reached by someone who was more competent at assessing immature ambition.

My resentment at this disappointment is still acute. I am convinced that had I on this occasion been snubbed in private for the futile lavishness of my essay and at the same time been encouraged to read and imitate the writers of simple English prose, I should have gained two years at least in literary awareness, and that my first year at Oxford would not have been the unhappy derelict that it became. Never have I been wholly able to catch up that first year when I drifted shy and rudderless. And I date this misfortune to the day when I was exposed to public ignominy for my essay on a piece of coal.

I do not wish to exaggerate the effect of these two humiliations or to convey the impression that at Wellington I was in any way unhappy or misunderstood. True it was that my inability to play games with that skill which might be expected from my sturdiness deprived me of the more glittering prizes of school eminence. Yet this has not left me with any disbelief in the value of athletics in the public school system. I approve, for many reasons, of the preponderating importance attached in any English school to games. Hero-worship is inseparable from early adolescence and, under cover of athleticism, it emerges at its least sickly. The thought of intellectual hero-worship turns me cold. And in the end, the balance adjusts itself. The athlete chews the cud of his old memories: the intellectual compensates for past humiliations by sneering at his old school.

Not that I should wish to sneer. I realize to-day that in my own case a certain faculty for merriment protected me against the effect, as even against the realization, of my own discomfiture. Never during all those years at a public school was I reduced to tears or even to morbid introspection; and how often, upon the pine-clad air, did my laughter ring out, not unrestrained merely, but even shared; but often encouraged. I may have been fortunate in my immediate surroundings: the house of Mr. Kempthorne was an admirable house; and Mr. Kempthorne himself — one of the most gentle gentlemen I have ever known — introduced in his absent-minded way a certain standard of civilization even among the savages that we were. Yet there are moments in the early dawn when I think back upon those years, and force myself to imagine what would have happened had I possessed less resilience of temperament, had Mr. Kempthorne and Dr. Pollock not been there. I can picture a situation in which all my better qualities would have been driven into hiding and in which my desire to please (not in itself a very discreditable desire) might have assumed unctuous and even tortuous forms. There are moments when I tremble for what might have happened to a person as sensitive, as short-sighted as, and less amused than, I was myself. Much as I dislike the weaker brethren, I am obliged to confess that the weak brother, had he not possessed my own adventitious protections, might, at the Wellington of 1904, have become permanently warped.

It was in such a mood of anxiety regarding the possible fate of my supposed counterpart that, but a few months ago, I revisited Wellington College. All seemed changed. A boy who possessed a taste for water-colours (a taste which in my day was firmly and rightly suppressed) was allowed to smear his washes to his heart's content, nor was any hint of insanity adduced to justify his taste. A boy who was interested in iambics was allowed without let or question to revel in his eccentricity. There was a faint breeze in the air from the olives of the Academe; the old pine-laden heartiness had lost its cruel tang.

One thing, however, did remain — a thing which I still regard as the main and the most stupid defect of the whole Wellingtonian system. In my day it was not thought proper that boys should become acquainted with other boys who were not in their own house or dormitory. The range of our acquaintance was thus limited to the thirty boys who happened to be housed under the same roof. Ten of these boys were too old, and ten too young, for intimacy. One's radius of friendship was thus reduced to ten companions. This reduction was most damaging, as I found to my bitter cost when I went up to Oxford. We learnt a great deal about Demosthenes and the Acts of the Apostles: we learnt but little about life. I thus found that my Etonian contemporaries at Oxford were at least two years more advanced than I was myself. That was a grave disability. This disability was due entirely to the Wellingtonian system and that system, I understand, is still based upon the theory that a housemaster wishes his boys to consort only with other boys with whom he is personally familiar. Here, once again, you have the typically English timidity in face of the unknown. Most (but not all) house-masters at Wellington would defend the system on the ground that it restricts opportunities for vice. I can assure them that in my day, the only result was to confine that vice (which is inevitable) into a narrow space where it became foetid, secretive and squalid to the last degree. Only by expansion and sublimation can that particular malady of adolescence be rendered healthy. We were all thrown back upon our miserable selves.

I have thus no affection for, no gratitude towards, my own old school. At most I can evoke a thin trickle of reminiscence — a memory of laughter and the wind in pine trees — a slight membrane of respect. A tiny rivulet in comparison to the Atlantic of veneration which I feel for Balliol. And why? Because Balliol was an intelligent institution. Whereas Wellington, in my day, was not. Had it not been for Dr. Pollock, Mr. Perkins and Mr. Kempthorne I should feel for Wellington little more than an irritated dislike. Yet these three men showed me, in their different ways, what a public school might mean to other people had it been a different public school. And to-day it is.

AN IRISH SCHOOLING

[Cork]

BY SEÁN O'FAOLÁIN

THE school I speak of was the Lancasterian School in the town of Cork, one of the first, and maybe the first, Bell and Lancaster schools founded in Ireland. This I did not discover, until long afterwards, for we all associated it with the enemies of the Tudors, and the good monks who taught us, being mentally and emotionally rather like children themselves, did not, I imagine, discover it at any time. It was originally a barrack or a poorhouse, or maybe a madhouse, but at any rate it was born weary like a Buddhist in his fourth transmigration, and should never have been used in our time for any purpose whatever. I do not know when it was founded, but I am certain that it defied all the change and alteration that overtook schooling since the days of Wordsworth, and I know that the hoary, dusty, cobwebbed atmosphere of the place remained to the end the atmosphere of Carleton rather than of Joyce — the atmosphere, that is, of an enormous hedge-school in what, so bizarre was the life there, must surely have been a discarded asylum.

At the centre of the school was the Big Room, what wealthier folk would have called the *Aula Maxima*. The roof was broken on either side of the roof-tree by a clerestory composed of hundreds upon hundreds of patches of glass; beneath this clerestory, 'dreadful and dizzy to cast one's eyes so low', four or five classes would 'toe the line' in different parts of the hall, curved about a horsehoe, chalked on the floor, at whose centre stood the black-robed monk in charge. Every second boy was barelegged, with the mud drying between his toes and zoomorphic tracery on his shins from sitting in the ashes of his laneway home. At playtime, when other classes were howling in the yard, we would stand thus, each boy with a little penthouse balanced on his head, an open book, to protect him from the penalty of falling glass. For the great game in the yard outside was what I have since heard called the Roof Game. It began with the throwing of a ball, a thing of paper and twine, sideways on the slates, and it ended with a mad tangle fighting under the gutters to catch the ball, when, where, and if it fell.

East and west were the aisles to this nave, sheltering one or two more classes each, as well as the science-room, which was also office, drawing-room, monks' lunch-room, and place of more painful and less modest corporal punishment. The Infants were tucked away behind the apse; there was a black-hole where chronic offenders were sometimes flung to whimper among the coals and the rats; a gravelled yard ran on each side of the building; the foul jakes lined it behind; and there was, finally, the caretaker's cottage where he stored thrown-out copy-books for fuel and broke up old desks for firewood.

I shall always associate this school with Lowood School in *Jane Eyre*, not because we ever had any Reverend Mr. Brocklehurst, but because in spite of much vermin, some disease, and no external beauty, in spite of the cold and the smells, we managed to create inside that crumbling hole a faery world of our own — and by *we*, I mean the monks and the children together, for these Brothers were truly brothers to us and I think we really loved them. They were country lads with buttermilk complexions, hats prevented from extinguishing their faces only by the divine prescience of ears, hands still rough from the spade and feet still heavy with the clay. I recall their complete lack of self-consciousness with us — which did not prevent them from being shy and blushing in the presence of other monks — the complete absence of the keep-the-boy-in-his-place rule which (perhaps largely in self-defence) is so common in High Schools. Some, to be sure, were disliked — it is not in the nature of small boys to hate — and because they were mincing or had no sense of fun we called them names like Cinderella or Sloppy Dan.

But in general it is their simplicity that I recall now, their jokes that were not made simple for our benefit but were born simple of simple parents, the games they played with us so lustily with bits of stick or cloth-balls in the rough yard, their inquisitiveness about our home lives, their natural piety that threw a benignity over all our days. I recall their general and particular ignorance with a general and particular delight. I once wrote a childish essay on Fishing

for my Brother Josephus in which I cheekily described how I went fishing up the Lee and fished
up a girl; and I still remember the utter joy with which
they all crowded about that essay, gloating in their
own knowledge of worldly wickedness. And, to reverse
the roles, how innocent Brother Patrick seemed to us
when he began to warn us about the great temptations
of the summer time and how he actually knew little
boys who went swimming without any bathing-
drawers at all! As they grew older and were instructed
better they gradually moved on to High School or
Secondary School where with the increase in their
'little learning' they often became priggish and un-
likeable; and they often became unhappy, and between comic and tragic like the two poor men, who
for all their thirty years or more we used to watch
throwing their eyes mawkishly after girls. One was
always hearing of this or that monk who left the
Order or was about to leave it, though I find it hard
to imagine how they could ever earn a living after
being so long cloistered away from the competing
world.

As to their particular ignorance, I remember it, I
hope, not with the slightest feeling of superiority but
because, even then we knew that their weight of
knowledge did not prevent them from being very near
our ignorance. They — the pronoun is colloquial and
exclusive — commonly mispronounced words and
place-names in frequent use, saying NewFOUNDland,
HanoVER, *coincīdence*; were free with superfluous
syllables as in *cathedaral*; failed to recess the accent as

in *contráry* — it is the natural conservatism of the provincial which still says *tay* for *tea*, that says *demónstrate* for *démonstrate*; they were hopelessly muddled by *shall* and *will*; the use of the Gaelic present-habitual for the English present, *They do be* for *They are*, was widespread, and so on — lapses which are all easily remembered because forgotten with difficulty among the 'little gents' of the higher school. I can scarcely believe my memory when I seem to recall being told by Brother Josephus that combustion is due to phlogiston; that Brother Philip told us that circumcision was a small circle cut out on the forehead of Jewish children; clearly his reading misled him; but I do know, having verified it by the memory of others, that we were told there were twelve minerals and we were given their names, and that was that. On the other hand I always think admiringly of old Brother Magnus, who offered sixpence to anybody who would extract salt from the seawater in the harbour, and when one or two did it, offered a silver watch to any boy who would extract sugar from a turnip.

The point is, we all worked together as in a family, conspiring for example against inspectors from the Board of Education, or even against the headmaster. I remember one Inspector of Hygiene who came to lecture us on cleanliness — a badly needed lecture in that school — about nails, and hair and teeth and soforth, while our Brother Josephus stood in the background with a slow smile about his lips. When the man of cleanliness was finished Josephus showed him out coldly and then, turning back to us, swept us together into his bosom for ever and ever in one wave of indignation by saying in contempt of all inspectors: 'Boys! He thinks ye're filth!' When more important inspectors were coming how we worked in preparation, often copying in reams from old boys' essays, in the full knowledge that it was all a 'racket'; and after the inspection, during which the poor little monks stood about pale and trembling, we would crowd about our particular Josephus to know if we had done well — well by him, that is — rejoicing if he told us mildly that we had done quite well, then pulling us up short in the sudden effort to recapture his sadly damaged authority.

I know I am doing them all an injustice, and doing those years an injustice too. It is another world, not only gone for ever now, but not to be recaptured even in memory. All I did and learned there was done and learned for the love of the thing. In the High School, life and learning became (and have ever since remained) complicated by the importunity of those two heritages of Adam, the conscience and the will. From that complicated world to look back on a world where these genii did not exist is to look into a blinding light. Life there was a succession of dream-days which now as a writer — self-conscious like all my tribe — I envy almost to tears, because they were the only days of my life that were really lived. Then there were, in our minds, no strivings towards an end, as in school later (or towards perfection, as in the conscience of the grown man, writer or artisan) to annotate the joys of living by reminders of the seriousness of life. Far otherwise, all the seriousness of life was annotated by the sheer, unconscious joy of being simply alive. I had not eaten of the apple of ambition and was unaware of nakedness.

Do not imagine that a child does not enjoy 'being simply alive', or that when a man says he recalls pleasant times at school that he means anything but times that seemed pleasant then. Indeed, the *recherche du temps perdu* is always melancholy with a sense of loss where the *temps* itself glowed with immediacy.

What of those wet Southern days when few children dared come to school and the feeling of comradeship among those that came was so great that we hated to return home? Where the rain lashed the patched windows in the clerestory and we crowded over the fire to talk of the tawny rivers of the city rising in flood! When we rounded our cheeks and rolled our eyes and said Oooh! to the wind under the door! Yes! One could weep now because never again can one say Oooh! to the wind under the door, but then it was all sheer delight in the delights of Delight itself. And then there were days before breaking-up at summer-time, when all fear of inspectors was vanished, and we did nothing for days but clean the white ink-wells, and roll up the maps, and disclose on the walls behind them sudden stored blasts of light, and shoved dusters down one another's backs, and crushed closer than ever about the skirts of the Brothers to talk of our home, and our holidays, and their homes and their holidays, and our future — which meant next year — and theirs that meant, alas, poor adults, so much more. You looked back at the last moment at the crumb-laden floors, and the dust under the desks, all empty, and you felt the crumbs at the bottom of your school-sack that suddenly having lost all its import smelt only of vanished days; and you turned away as to a long exile.

It's the sense of wonder which is gone now, I suppose, the capacity of enjoyment killed by constant ratiocination, by too much thinking of things instead of doing them. Even those casualties from falling glass, or stones flung in yard-fights, were welcome because you were led out by an elder boy to be stitched or bandaged at the hospital, a pleasantly terrifying experience, during which you wondered if you were really going to die. These breaks were typical of that school; it was a delight to be sent making up the rolls, doing all the adding and subtracting and compiling that the Head was too lazy to do himself; to be sent out to the street just before roll-call to see if any laggards were coming, in which case you certainly told the shivering wretch that Sloppy Dan would KILL him when he got inside; magical to be sent in search of a missing pupil down among the penthouse lanes of the city, in and out of Featherbed or Cut-throat where the shifts and shawls drying from window to window made the colours of a canopy in a papal procession, where every dark doorway under the thatch, shot by its blob of fire-light, delayed further your already slow-lingering steps.

One may think that it was not a good school, but I think it was — fairly good. Its great drawback was that a clever boy fell at once into habits of idleness there for lack of competition; the pace was set, perforce, for slowcoaches. But the great point about the place was that it was not even faintly 'respectable' and though the teaching was serious it was never solemn. We learned there that learning can be an interesting occupation, and we learned to enjoy without question, as equals, one another's company. When I think of the other kind of school, your High, Secondary, or Public School, where the little gentlemen are critical of one another without rest, and think of learning only as a means to an end, I sigh with relief at being free of it as one sighs on waking from a painful dream.

Not that my school was not cold and cheerless and had not some bad hours. I can never forget that one or two of these monks were rude, brutal men who terrified the very heart out of us at times. I am thinking particularly of one huge fellow in the Third, or Fourth class, I forget which, who had a throat and a voice like a bull, and a strong right arm coming down with the leather-strap, half an inch thick, on our palms. He used, at one period, to collect bread from the monks' lunch-room, and after school set two of his bigger boys, newsboys by night, school-children by day, fighting with bare fists and bare to the waist, for these scraps of food; and withheld the bread one afternoon because they were either not hungry enough, or were too hungry, to take part in his circus. I saw him in the street, years later, when I was in the University, and I looked at his dark jowl with sideward glance, almost in fear.

The place is gone now; not a stone remains upon a stone, and a boot factory in red brick stands where it stood. A new, modern school replaces it, all white tiles and parquet, very anodyne and aseptic. That is all to the good, but it is not that which gives it an advantage over the old place. It is beside fields, and below it there are trees through which one sees the flowing river with cows in other fields beyond. In our old place there were a few ragged trees growing out of asphalt but not a blade of grass to be seen anywhere; and a school without a field is a prison.

If I were child again and both schools stood, to which would I go? If not to some sterner, more ambitious school than either of them? It is a question *à hausser les épaules*. Certainly, if it is a matter of getting on in the world, to neither. But if one places more value on other things, then this type of school is ideal, and according as you value these 'other things' the more, then the more reason to go to some old shack like mine where, although one learned little about the world, one imbibed a great deal about life — and perhaps a little about the next life, too.

THE GOTHIC ARCH

[Rugby]

BY WILLIAM PLOMER

I

I AM not one of those who regard the Old School and its institutions as fixed in a sacred unchangeableness. However much I should like to be able to respect order, authority and tradition, and to adopt a 'catholic' attitude, I often find myself committed to a 'protestant' one. I feel a deep discontent with many of the things I was brought up to take for granted as being wise, useful, and necessary. The reasons for this discontent may no doubt be discovered in my own character. I suppose I was not an 'average' boy (if such an extraordinary phenomenon exists) and I know that my generation grew up in peculiar circumstances: our schooling was much affected and mine was broken off short by the War.

It seems clear that to question a firmly-established form of education is to question the civilization it is intended to foster. Poke your finger into that hornet's-nest of a topic, the public school, and the air is at once full of the wings and stings of the enemies of change and the angry buzzings of outraged nitwits. It also seems clear that the public school cannot be considered apart from the preparatory school and the university — are they to be exempt from what the Americans call a probe?

With a view to my getting a sound, ordinary education I was sent, nearly twenty years ago, to a preparatory school in the south. Now just the other day I was reading some reminiscences by Mr. Norman Douglas, in which he has described his own impressions of a preparatory school. All this was interesting to me not only as a sketch of a Victorian preparatory school by a man of the world who is also a scholar and a wit, but because I suddenly felt convinced that there was some close connection between my school and his. Possibly the later school was in some way an offshoot of the earlier, or the clergyman who kept my school may have been a master at his, as I believe was the case: I certainly recollect stray references to Mr. Douglas's school and also a framed water-colour of that establishment. I cannot pretend to feel much warmer about my school than Mr. Douglas does about his. I did not see at the time, and I do not see now, why life should be like the life I had to lead there and was asked to believe in. I do not understand why the energy and joyfulness of the young should be so largely wasted, or why a civilization which has produced Chaucer and Shakespeare and Herrick and Keats should be turned into something extremely sour and ugly. At my school I received the impression that the ritual of the cricket field, more elaborate and just a trifle more sincerely performed than that of the chapel, was equally religious, and that pleasure must necessarily always be wrong unless it happens to coincide with what one's enemies regard as duty. Not, I think, especially unamiable by nature, why was I taught to hate, with a hearty and enduring hatred, the constricted life of the school and most of the settled convictions that determined it?

On still days, when we were bent over Livy or quadratic equations, the windows would be rattled by a sudden crescendo of the interminable thunder of the guns in Flanders, and a wandering breeze would stir the war-map on the wall, where little flags on pins marked the graph of the Western Front and, to the east, the progress of what the newspapers called 'the Russian steam-roller'; we were still being taught to believe in and serve the 'ideals' that were destroying the generation a little older than our own, the generation of Wilfred Owen.

In the holidays I spent much of my time in military hospitals and canteens, in the company of wounded soldiers, whom I did my best to help or amuse. 'Theirs but to do and die,' we learnt at school — and ours, too. But why? What for? At one moment we might be listening in chapel to the Sermon on the Mount; at another we might be watching bayonet practice on the common, where overgrown errand boys in khaki were being taught by a sergeant to stab sacks filled with straw and painted with a rough likeness of the Kaiser. I do not say that we boys were unaffected by the war-fever, nor do I say that at the time I was able to explain my feelings to myself as I have explained them since. What I do say is that powerful feelings were there in my heart, of resentment against those who taught me and their teachings, and of pity for the wounded soldiers, of sympathy and love, as if I were on their side, somehow taking their part against the huge forces that had filled this man's lungs with gas, driven this one mad, and torn away that one's genitals. *Onward, Christian soldiers,* we sang in chapel.

What can I say in favour of this school? I enjoyed one of my punishments, which was the getting by heart of a good many lines of Virgil. I might have enjoyed the swimming, only the bath was shut in by trees, and the water looked like cold strong tea and was full of newts, leaves, slime and tadpoles. But in the winter we sometimes got some skating or went tobogganing, and in the summer we helped once or twice with the haymaking. Cigarettes tasted nicer to me than perhaps they ever have since, and when I was head prefect I enjoyed undermining the authority of the headmaster as far as I could. He could not conceal his surprise when I took quite a high place in the Common Entrance examination. I believe he thought I was just a fribble, but if so he was an inexact judge of character. Of course, I refer to the school as it seemed to me then; I believe it no longer exists.

11

By the time I got to Rugby the War was no longer being regarded quite so light-heartedly as in the song:

> 'Hats off to Tommy Atkins
> Taking his chance,
> On duty with the Blankshires
> Somewhere in France.'

The lengthening casualty lists, the air raids, the submarine warfare, and the shortage of food scarcely encouraged optimism. Wherever you went, the War was with you. On the station platform at Rugby, one of the longest in England, there were no porters, and the boys returning to school had to shift their own luggage.

One's first days at a public school do not allow one to think much of international events, and for new boys trifles are important. Having taken Greek in the Common Entrance I had been posted to the classical side, but meant to go on the modern. A fearful confusion resulted, and I wandered in and out of classrooms where I did not belong, occasionally seeking the guidance of a sort of commissionaire, an individual who (I learnt later) used to prepare boys for a birching with the comforting words, ''Tain't the hagony, it's the disgrace': a true supporter, evidently, of the public school code, he failed to realize that where there is any disgrace in flogging it is more than likely to rest with those who sanction or administer it. I soon began to get used to the routine and the elaborate system of taboos, both official and unofficial, by which the life of the boys was governed. But I cannot say that I was unhappy, for I was enjoying a little more freedom than I had been used to at my preparatory school.

I do not know if the system of fagging at Rugby was peculiar to that school. A prefect or somebody would stand bawling for a fag, then all the little boys would go scuttling down passages and stairs to answer the call, and the last one to arrive would be given some task to do. This seemed to me so silly that I never bothered to leave my study, and was never found out. Perhaps this behaviour, combined with my distaste for games, drilling, and various other activities, may help to make me appear a lazy shirker, but the truth is I am and always have been energetic when interested — I might even have answered a fag-call by a prefect whom I should have liked to be of service to, and I should have taken care to arrive last.

During the War, schoolmasters were often either dotards or weaklings, and I do not suppose that the sadism and the lack of warmth, imagination, modesty and culture which they so often exhibit were in those days any less in evidence than usual. At Rugby there was the rufous, peppery X; the hearty Y, with his mania for cold baths and early morning runs and his habit of speaking of 'a slab of poetry'; and the wretched harassed, henpecked Z, who could never keep order. But there were also Dr. David and Mr. B. The last-named taught French, and taught it well, according to a method of his own which made for fluency rather than precision. In my first term, insignificant and bewildered, I was very pleasantly surprised to receive from Mr. B an invitation to a tea-party to be given in honour of my birthday. I feel that this invitation was a recognition of my existence as a human being. Mr. B had a wife and child and a pleasant house. He had also a handsome head with a wing of grey hair brushed back on either side. This head was full of ideas. There was intelligence in every line of his face, and in some of the lines there were cruelty, a cynical wit, and kindness as well. I could not understand how such a brilliant and amiable a person as he seemed to me could ever have become a master in a public school, a man so full of curiosity and up-to-date knowledge. He told me on my birthday that he had just had a letter from the London library complaining that he had taken out no less than sixty books. He had asked to meet me three of the most agreeable of my contemporaries, and we used afterwards to meet at his house quite often. He encouraged us to think, we read papers on subjects that interested us, and I showed him some verses I had written.

Dr. David, now Bishop of Liverpool, was the head-master and also my house-master. A tall, dark man with a rugged, ascetic-looking face, he has not gone through life satisfied with things as he has found them. I remember not long ago examining a photograph of a concourse of Anglican bishops. There they sat, row upon row, like a school of sleek sea-monsters washed up on the rocks, their faces mostly wearing an expression of blank complacency and self-importance as if the world depended on them. It seemed extraordinary that these pink magnates should have anything to do with people's souls, and as I looked at the photograph I remembered that they had nothing to do with mine nor, I thought, with those of anybody I loved or respected. Good and honest creatures some of them may have been, but some of those faces were undisguisedly worldly. Here the big belly seemed to hang suspended from the narrow mind, like a soap-bubble from a clay pipe; here professional kindliness or archness swam like oil on the surface of intolerance;

here was the hatchet-face of one whose life had been devoted to being on the safe side; here was some bluff eunuch who would use in the pulpit metaphors inspired by cricket, regarding life as one vast game in which, by keeping a straight bat and following that variety of the herd-instinct called the team-spirit, he had managed to pile up a tidy score — 'Well played, sir!' I felt constrained to murmur . . . But among all those faces one face stood out. It seemed to me the face of an exceptional man and an exceptional Christian, as long before it had seemed the face of an exceptional schoolmaster. Naturally I remember its owner with gratitude and respect, for although I had little direct contact with him he treated me as an individual, not just as one of six hundred Rugbeians. He lent me out of his own library a book by Turgenev (imagine that, the head master of one of our Great Public Schools lending a boy of fourteen a book by a Russian novelist!) and when my existence began to be affected by special circumstances he gave them the most careful and sympathetic consideration. Owing to those special circumstances I eventually left the school before I had done my time, but I did not leave, I am afraid, under anything so picturesque as a cloud.

I do not remember ever having played a game of either cricket or football at Rugby. I cannot account for this, because games were compulsory and I was not excused from playing them. Perhaps I did play and have forgotten. Certainly I had already spent a good part of several years of my life keeping balls out of goals and away from wickets or propelling them towards those structures, though I never cared twopence whether they reached them or not. I had played endless cricket at my preparatory school, and I bowled with some effect in such a baroque style that nobody knew which way the ball would break, and I sometimes had doubts myself; at football I had played for the school and we sometimes won matches against other schools. If I found games boring that does not mean that at Rugby I was immobile in my spare time. I did a good deal of running, and also took part in the activities of the Officers' Training Corps, which, being in those days a preparation for the trenches, was taken pretty seriously. I led, in fact, a very active life indoors and out, but now we come to the point that I was not able to sustain it.

Certainly I was sound, as they say, in wind and limb, and had nothing much wrong with me but a weakness of the eyes. But I was beginning to outgrow my strength, and suffered from under-nourishment. We were all on rations. Little slices of chilled meat, a small quantity of doubtful bread, and a few spoonfuls of sugar — those had to last a week. I can remember working all the morning on a winter's day, then sitting down to a little slop of bony boiled fish and a dab of watery custard, and then working again, going out for a long run in the afternoon, and working again at night. We were allowed, I think, an extra half hour in bed in the mornings to help to make up for the shortage of food. But I was often hungry, and semi-starvation and puberty and too much form-work by artificial light began to tell on me, and every time I

saw the oculist he found my eyes growing weaker.
Dr. David allowed me to give up some of my classes
and also to resign from the Corps.

Having time on my hands, I got a bicycle and went
out into the surrounding country. During the War
the country, in the absence of men and traffic, was
peaceful as it has never been since. Certainly its
peacefulness was not free from melancholy, and there
was always tension in the air, and sometimes an
aeroplane or even a Zeppelin as well. The quietness
of Newbold or Hillmorton or Dunchurch or Ashby St.
Ledgers or Kenilworth in those summer days of 1918
was almost eerie. When the wind seemed suddenly to
catch the willows of a water-meadow in a silver net,
tugging them sideways against a stormy background,
rustling the ivy on a ruin, and shifting the fragrance
of meadow-sweet and water-mint, or when a shaft of
late sunlight slanted upon some tomb or memorial
urn in a quiet, musty church, surrounding with its
radiance the kneeling alabaster children of some Jaco-
bean squire, all rendered headless by Puritan zeal —
at such times the atmosphere seemed to be that of an
earlier age. Fresh and tranquil, the countryside had
an air of slightly ominous innocence, as in the land-
scapes of Constable and Cotman, and leaning against an
old oaken pew and looking at the trunks of those young
people in ruff and doublet or deep-folded gown, one could
well suppose that it was really little more than a hundred
years since Cromwell's men had beheaded them.

The acute sense of the past which I had at that time
may have been partly due to the fact that my blood

was by no means foreign to that midland soil — a namesake and ancestor of mine, for instance, was at Rugby in the seventeenth century, and on my mother's side I am descended from the Ardens, a family who lived in Warwickshire from ancient times. But if in the stillness, the magic suspense, of that war-time countryside an instinctive *nostalgie du passé* seemed to evoke with no little power the very atmosphere of the past, I would not deny that incongruities were present. The telegraph wires did not forget to hum; on my way to the fields, I might have to pass through the industrial squalor of New Bilton and might later catch sight, in the blue and bosky distance, of the smoking chimneys of Coventry; and a long procession of army lorries, like migrating monsters, would appear on a high road. In a lane I met a German prisoner driving a farm cart and sucking a straw, somebody's blue-eyed boy,

'And his teeth made for laughing round an apple.'

With him I exchanged on more than one occasion a few phrases of class-room German and a handclasp, wondering if the adjectives were agreeing with the nouns and feeling pleasure, not the less keen because it was secret, at a human contact which seemed to make the War a half-forgotten bad dream.

I made some study of local history, finding the school library helpful, and even compiled a little monograph about a hamlet on the Avon, including in it an account of a murder that took place there long ago. Was it not a certain Theodosius Boughton who poisoned a Captain Donnellan, his sister's lover, with laurel-water? How much more real it was to me than the tedious banality of everyday life at school! And it was perhaps this taste for local history that led me to look at country churches with an enthusiasm fanned by the worthy Bloxam, who had himself lived at Rugby, and had conveniently classified church architecture as Saxon, Norman, Early English, Decorated, and Perpendicular. Instinctively I preferred the round arch to the pointed one, the affinities of my nature possibly being more with the Romanesque kind of civilization than with the Gothic, more Southern than Northern. What a relief it was to get away from the hideousness of Rugby Chapel and the striped brick-work of Butterfield's quadrangle, and to stand and look at or touch with my hand the bold Norman curve, yellowed and slightly distorted, of the chancel-arch at Stoneleigh. I shall never forget the pure excitement that the sight of some old round arch could give me in those days, and I remember later, when I was very ill with Spanish influenza, how such an image continually haunted me in delirium. I think of it now as a symbol of the life I did not relinquish, and of the life I believe in. I should like my life to make such a curve, solidly built, boldly patterned, set in its proper place, upholding a weight, and affording entrance to further developments. None of your Gothic rhapsodies for me, your ogees and crockets and heavenward soarings.

As I afterwards became a writer, it interests me to recall my approaches to the enjoyment and practice of literature. One of my form-masters commended my essays but found fault with a tendency I had to use rather long, Johnsonian words of Latin derivation. 'Good English,' he said, 'is written with Anglo-Saxon monosyllables.' The use of the word 'monosyllable' rather weakened a pronouncement which may have had some value as a corrective, but was obviously absurd as an opinion. A language so rich and re-sourceful as ours deserves more discerning use than a style which steals its thunder from the spelling book or the quaint archaisms of William Barnes. I remember we were 'taught' a good deal of Tennyson and William Morris and a book by Mr. Hilaire Belloc. *Georgian Poetry* must have been still too daring and advanced for the class-room. In the school library, however, I routed out a little edition of *The Marriage of Heaven and Hell*. Like the discovery of Rimbaud a year or two later, it was so exciting that it used to keep me awake at night.

But in the meantime it had become impossible for me to go on with my school work, and as the oculist thought I ought to live in the open air, I was obliged to leave Rugby. As I drove to the station, a column of American soldiers was marching through the streets.

III

After I left school I was sent to live on a farm in the wilds of Berkshire. There was an old labourer I used sometimes to work with, and I remember how uneasy I felt with him at first. He was, I think, a person of solid character, kind, sensible and placid, but I could scarcely understand a word of his broad local speech and my own way of talking seemed to me and perhaps to him over-refined and slightly condescending in tone, though I had no wish to condescend or to be thought condescending. I was not in the position of a person giving orders, and it seemed absurd that there should not be a feeling of ease between two fellow-countrymen standing side by side on the same soil, whatever the differences in their age, class, background, and education. I was very glad when the difficulties of communication began to diminish.

When there was a shoot I used to go sometimes with the beaters instead of the guns, and it was then that I met a man of about thirty who now seems to me to have been not altogether unlike some gamekeeper or other out of the novels of D. H. Lawrence. He seemed to feel rather brotherly and protective towards me, and was by no means without experience. Instead of treating me like a 'gentleman' he treated me as a boy who did not want to feel lonely and needed the kindness and affection of an older man. He provided me with that kindness and affection in a more direct and comforting way than any schoolmaster ever did. He could not have taught me chemistry or French idioms but he did awaken in me some feeling for the actualities of life, and if circumstances had not separated us would have probably influenced or educated me to no small extent.

This is not the place to describe my later fortunes, but rather to compare my broken school-career with the careers of those who have been through the whole sequence of preparatory school, public school and university from start to finish. I am inclined to think that as I went 'out into the world' rather early I did

not remain schoolboyish so long as some do. By the
time I was seventeen I was earning my living: in the
employed classes that would not be remarkable, but
in the employing classes it is unusual. Although I
dare say the advantages and disadvantages of attending a university or going out into the world may on
the whole be about equal, I feel that as far as I am
concerned the main things I missed by not going up
to Oxford were the chance of making some good
friends, the chance of working out in conversation
with people of my own sort a lot of ideas that I have
had to grapple with by myself, and a training in
methods of thought. But when I look round, after
living in various places and among a great variety of
people, at English public school boys and men I am
often struck by their puerility, their dreary philistin-
ism, their ignorance of things which seem to me important or interesting, and their strong herd-instinct.
I read last year in a newspaper[1] an interesting letter from
Colonel Arthur Osburn. He said that if boys:

> 'are ever to grow into men, sixteen should be the
> leaving age at school and nineteen for a university.
> Even so some of the most impressionable years will
> have been wasted learning competitive games and
> indulging in flogging smaller boys. The sooner a
> youth learns to think and act and fend for himself
> as an equal amongst equals and not as a docile
> fag or privileged prefect the better for himself
> and everyone else.'

This seems sound. After all, life is very short. Why

[1] The *Sunday Referee*.

should a man spend nearly a quarter of a century in being 'educated'? The result is often an arrested development, and, as Colonel Osburn remarked, stultification, and the 'Third Form stupidity and Sixth Form arrogance that landed us in the Boer War . . . and the political insanity of the Black-and-Tan imbroglio in Ireland', beside the 'schoolboy silliness and bluff that caused the General Strike, and the "Play the Game" attitude,' which, he says, helped to make the Great War inevitable.

There are probably still plenty of people who say that their schooldays were the best time of their lives. But I cannot see that hors d'oeuvres are the best part of a meal, or that we should eat so much of them that we are left with no time or room for the soup and the fish. I think that education, like hors d'oeuvres, should whet the appetite for what is to follow. I think it should help people to work hard at things they want to do and are fitted to do, and that they should not be pestered or brutalized with irrelevant drudgery and petty tyranny. I cannot see why boys should not be made as happy as possible, for in my experience people are better when they are happy, and to be happy is not necessarily to be, as schoolmasters seem to think, a spineless hedonist. If the Old School could do something more than it does at present to further these aims, to weaken the prejudices of the mass and cherish and develop the individual, who gives life to civilization — well, I believe I wouldn't mind being seen occasionally in an Old School tie, though as a matter of fact I don't much care for stripes.

THE WAT'RY GLADE

[Eton]

BY ANTHONY POWELL

THE day after my arrival at Eton, finding some time
to myself, I was making use of it by looking out of the
window in the hope of seeing something of interest, a
bad habit which I have never been able to overcome.
My room was small and had a sloping roof and no
lock on the door, but it seemed a scarcely credible
haven of privacy after the communal life to which I
had been accustomed. It was a summer afternoon
and the window opened on to a quiet street with red
houses opposite. A boy of about fifteen was walking
slowly along on the far side of the road with one hand
in his pocket and the other supporting a pile of books,
which rested like a field-marshal's bâton against his
thigh. His top hat was at the back of his head and he
wore exceptionally short trousers and light-coloured
socks. One of his shoulders was higher than the other
and a slight sag at the knees made him an almost
perfect specimen of the world-famous Eton-slouch.
While he walked he whistled. The tune was the chorus
of a then popular song, the words of which, so far as I
can remember, went:

K-K-K-Katie, beautiful Katie,
You're the only g-g-g-girl that I adore;
When the m-m-m-moon shines
On the c-c-c-cowshed
I'll be waiting at the k-k-k-kitchen door.

This was the most sophisticated thing I had ever seen. I realized all at once that the boy was a figure from a new world. First impressions are important and all this elegance gave me at an early stage in my career a conception of the school of which I was never able to divest myself entirely. I felt that at last I was among men. Later on in the half I coxed a boat for two of the more senior members of my house. Their manner and the terms with which they greeted disobliging circumstances confirmed me in this opinion. Many of the phrases used by them were still unfamiliar, but the words had a vigour which demanded immediate respect. There was a certainty about the standards of the people I found myself among which was to make the assurance even of undergraduates seem vapid and self-conscious.

To give an exact picture of life at Eton would be no easier than to give an exact picture of how human beings behave in trains or on board ship or at the cinema or any other place where time, space and convention impose certain well-defined bounds. Obviously all persons engaged in any of these occupations have a good deal in common just as all Etonians wore top hats and, when they were tall enough, tail coats and white ties and went to early school and had their names called out at Absence. But beyond all these things was their individual experience which in a school of eleven hundred boys differed considerably, as widely as that of persons who, seeing the same film, laugh, weep, sleep, try to think out their business problems or make love to their neighbour; during the same voyage, are seasick or flourish on the ozone; and travelling behind the same engine spend their time in a *wagon-lit*, the dining-car or the lavatory. This fact is seldom pondered by the swarm of indignant Peter Pans who lie for ever in ambush with pens in their hands, ready to contradict any statement about any school that may seem to have the appearance of a generalization. For their benefit I have tried to make any impression that I may succeed in giving of Eton, Eton seen palpably through my own eyes; and I must apologize to others who, for this reason, may find the picture obtrusively personal.

My private school had reflected in some degree the atmosphere, if not the conditions, of Dotheboys Hall. Mollycoddling notions had inevitably crept in with the passage of time but in spite of these the traditions of the parent foundation had been never entirely lost sight of. I know that almost everyone holds the theory that his own preparatory school was less inviting than that to which anyone else was ever sent. This view might indeed be described as the Private School Spirit. I am no exception; but in justice to the institution itself and to my estimation of it, I should add that I arrived there in the middle of the War. Its headmaster had combined the aspect and political outlook of Mr. Rudyard Kipling with an inability to control his temper which might have been amusing enough in an acquaintance or a subordinate but was more than a little disconcerting in someone who for two-thirds of the year was in a position to exercise almost absolute authority over oneself. I did not care for him, nor for his school, and sometimes on icy football fields and during shifts of slave-labour when we chopped wood in his garden, I was almost inclined to doubt his often-repeated assertion that life was worse in the trenches. Flanked on one side by the disagreeable ghosts of this man and his seedy staff and on the other by the querulous phantoms that loom up out of the mists of Oxford, Eton stands, a florid interlude, coloured by a sort of hobgoblin realism like a picture by Brueghel.

I had the good fortune to be sent to a very 'bad' house. It was in fact, I do not think any of my contemporaries would dispute, the 'worst' house in the school. That is to say we had not survived the first round of the football ties for more than ten years and the only cup for competitive merit on our dining-room table was that awarded to the winning singing quartet. Worse still, there had been a period in the immediate past, happily drawing to a close at the time of my arrival, when the non-Aryan proportion in its membership had seemed to many unnecessarily high. The rest of the school looked upon us with great disfavour and it was at first a little alarming for newcomers to discover how great a load of disrespect had been inherited by them. But it was not long before most of them realized that they were in luck and I do not think that there were many, even among the ambitious, who would seriously have preferred to be in another house.

The building itself, of red brick, and like a clinic, stood on the south-west edge of the school by a field from which in winter a white vapour rose at night-time and veiled all but the upper stories. Unlike many of the houses, more attractive outside but startlingly medieval within, it possessed several bathrooms, while the six best rooms in the house had bow-windows with seats built into them. In these sybaritic surroundings, aggravated by a record of only moderate athletic success, it was not to be wondered at that its members showed an individuality that was considered in some quarters highly objectionable. In addition to this was the unusual personality of my house-master, whom I recall with affection, bursting like a sea-lion into boys' rooms when they least expected him, playing the Wall Game with almost homicidal violence, giving imitations of Mr. Gladstone, performing on the harmonium at prayers in the evening while we sang *All things Bright and Beautiful*, or hurrying feverishly through the passages with some huge volume illustrating the history of Footgear through the ages.

Perhaps it is important that those who have charge of the young should have peculiar mannerisms and eccentricities of appearance. The inexperienced can learn more easily from those who live their lives in the way that 'ham' actors play their parts. There was a long-standing tradition at Eton that masters should be a little odd, so that the school was on the whole admirably staffed. Teaching was efficient and it was assumed, or so it seemed to me, that every boy would at one time or another be in some such position as viceroy of India and must be brought up with this end in view. By this I do not mean that methods were very different from any other school. This impression is not easy to explain or to express in a few words. The government of the country was somehow made almost a personal matter. It was as if, instead of saying, 'If you don't learn to speak French properly, you will never be able to enjoy yourself in Paris,' our mentors said: 'If you don't learn some sort of civilized behaviour, England will become uninhabitable for everybody.' The psychological effect of this on boys of widely different character and mental capacity would make an interesting study, as it was a teaching that might produce anything from industrious civil servants to megalomaniac noblemen or industrious noblemen to megalomaniac civil servants. Examples of such types may be found by those who have the curiosity to examine old school lists; and lots of specimens in between, many of them well worth attention. Nothing could be further from the truth than the legend that no work was ever done, and the time spent in school or in pupil-room, especially by lower-boys, was long enough to satisfy any arm-chair-pedagogue. It is true that sometimes masters proved unequal to the gruelling course they had to run and left to be cabinet ministers or to become political bosses in truculent Balkan kingdoms, spheres where the maintenance of discipline came easily after what they had been through. But the days were long past when the headmaster, addressing the school, could say that he expected a volley of books when he left the room but he protested against the stone which had been aimed at him on the previous afternoon.

In my day no one ever dreamt of throwing stones at the headmaster. There was, in fact, very little opportunity for most of the school to do so, unless they had brought one into chapel, because although he could be seen walking about at cricket matches, chewing a daisy, many of the boys never came in contact with him at all. I myself only spoke to the headmaster a few times when I was on the Bill for minor offences, and all most of us knew about him was that he had a good appearance and a whimsical, rather swaggering dignity. He was also an amateur of the intellectual wisecrack and he used to write detective stories and preach luscious sermons on the subject of talks he had had with King Henry VI. After delivering these he would go and kneel at the end of the chapel, under the threatening tints of the East window, and I would be fascinated watching the broad rubber circles on the soles of his boots. The school never felt quite sure about him; but no books were thrown.

In saying that I never had anything to do with the headmaster beyond accepting a few hundred lines from him and listening to a confirmation talk at his house on the subject of Temptation, I do not wish to imply that there was any reason why contact between us should have been any closer. The whole of my life at Eton was spent in well-deserved obscurity. I have no triumphs to look back on and I think myself lucky to have reached at last the House Library, a room given over to about half a dozen boys at the top of the house, who were allowed certain privileges to compensate for the worries of being in a responsible position. It was a self-elected body and the captain of the house, who was chosen by each house-master and was not necessarily the highest up in school order, was its *ex-officio* president. It was reached by position in the school, ability to play games, and racketeering methods. Thus a clever but neurotic and unpopular boy would probably not be a member of the Library, while a really bestially stupid athlete might also find himself excluded. It was, however, possible for someone like myself, quite ludicrously bad at games and none too high up in the school, to achieve this distinction by intrigue on the part of friends.

The Library in my house was a fairly large room, containing several broken-down wicker arm-chairs, a table, a gramophone, an ottoman in which a collection of canes was kept and a few shelves of books. The books, on the whole, were a poor collection. The only one of any interest was called *Gutter Tragedies*. It was absorbing and made up for the deficiency of the other volumes. There were house-groups round the walls and a photogravure of *The Empty Chair* over the fireplace. This subsequently got broken in pieces and burnt, being replaced by some Aubrey Beardsley reproductions which went well with the photographs of Old Boys. The chief privilege of members of the Library was that, while each of them possessed one or more fags, they were also allowed to shout for all the lower-boys in the house, who had to run to this summons, the last one to arrive doing the task. Fagging at my house was never a very serious business. In this respect, too, we must have been exceptionally easy-going because I have heard boys in other houses complain that their first few terms were spent in doing a succession of odd-jobs. It was certainly annoying to have to jump up in the middle of work or reverie and be sent, when it was raining or oppressively hot, with a note folded up in the shape of a cocked-hat, to a boy in another house, but the system will no doubt continue until a telephone service is installed in each boy's room. In a conservative school like Eton this may not be for years, and accordingly time will be wasted. I should find it very irksome now to run errands or to make toast for persons older and more successful than myself, prosperous authors, for example like Mr. J. B. Priestley or Mr. Warwick Deeping, but I do not think that at the age of thirteen or fourteen my life was soured by its equivalent. Whatever the future holds in store, however much money is made, who again will be in a position to summon by a shout fifteen servants who know that physical agony will be the price of disobedience? None of us. The memory of past servitude seems a small thing by comparison.

Beatings took place in the Library. On the whole

they were rare, many including myself escaping entirely. They were usually inflicted for habitual ragging. They increased perceptibly during my middle period under a captain of games who had ideas about pulling the house together in the field of sport, a region in which he himself was fated to get into warm water later in life. When I was in the library we tried to dispense altogether with this form of discipline but unsuccessfully. The house showed signs of becoming a bear-garden. On one occasion we beat a boy on a frivolous charge. He was technically in the wrong but he would have got off if his general behaviour had not seemed insufferable. He was the son of a missionary and used to go about the house trying to do good. I am ashamed of this episode, having been in some degree a party to it, although the actual executive agent was the captain of the house, a great friend of mine, who for some unaccountable reason wore a dressing-gown throughout the proceedings, and I hope that if our victim has not long since been eaten by savages he will take this as some sort of public amends and bear only a reasonable amount of malice.

Just as the House Library was self-elected and was in control of the discipline of each house, the Eton Society, or Pop as it was called, a body of about thirty important-looking boys, acted in the same capacity for the school as a whole. They were allowed, among other privileges, to wear coloured waistcoats and snow-boots and to put sealing-wax seals on their hats. These may seem small things now but they did not at the time. The society had been founded at the beginning of the nineteenth century as a debating club for the school's highbrows, though it had been customary to elect the Captain of Boats to show that no animus was felt against athletics. In the course of time, like the Royal Academy, it had grown into something a little different from what had been intended at the outset, and although the election of a boy undistinguished athletically was by no means unknown, an accumulation of the right colours (the simile still holds) was the surest means of getting there. On the whole Pop was respected and its membership was considered life's highest ambition, but, like everything else at Eton — and I think this is an important point about the place as a school — Pop was not for this reason regarded as above criticism. During the Peace celebrations in the summer of 1919, towards the end of my first half, Pop tried to enforce an order forbidding boys to cross the bridge to Windsor or something of the sort. Precisely what they had to do I cannot remember but I know that the more discreet members of the society stayed in their houses. The others ran aimlessly about, slashing at some of the smaller boys with the nobbly canes they carried, quite unable to cope with a situation of which their prestige should have made them complete masters. I even saw a row of lower-boys strolling along arm-in-arm, an intimacy Pop arrogated to themselves and the friends with whom they walked. It was while linked in this very way to his betters that a boy, not himself a member of Pop but hoping for speedy election by taking their side, had his head cut open by half a brick, thrown, I believe, by an Australian soldier during the goings-on. Some time later he was elected (the sycophant, not the soldier) so it must have been worth it in the long run.

As I never made a century at Lords nor rowed in the winning crew for the Ladies' Plate, I can only imagine the degree of such pleasurable memories. The sensations of those to whom after an important match the Keeper of the Field threw, ever so non-chalantly, his cap must have been extremely enjoyable. Probably winners of a Newcastle Scholarship, even, felt quite pleased with themselves. For my part I cannot say that I envy any of them. My own quieter recollections are no less agreeable. Going down 'after twelve' to Tap, a sort of pub which was in bounds and where excellent savouries could be bought to blunt the appetite for Boys' Dinner; playing poker in m'Dame's room on winter evenings, even though I never held any cards; pottering about the drawing schools and hearing about a painter called Matisse; or taking a rigger up the river to Queen's Eyot and having tea and lying in the sun. The days, lasting up to the 'seventies, were over when Etonians had rambled about the country in search of wild flowers, a congenial pursuit which ignorance of all forms of botany would have prevented me from indulging in, but an occasional Russian cigarette was never more pleasant than when smoked in a ditch on Dawnay Common when spring had begun in the hedges. There were some of the buildings, the view that Canaletto painted, for instance, though where exactly he sat I have never been able to decide, and the trees of Upper Club and wandering about School Library, and those rare visits to out-of-bounds cinemas where the entertainment seemed so much better than any films seen since; while half a bottle of Graves for lunch at Henley lies deeper than mere sentiment, the first taste of those acid, savourless vintages that fall to the lot of the indigent. I like to remember the melancholy fields that skirt the Sewage Farm across which we used to return from beagling, hoping that the boy we messed with had not forgotten to get the sausages for tea, or brooding on romantic agitations of the moment which seem in retrospect so extravagant. The very last thing in the world I should wish would be to become a boy again but I know that some of these moments were not so bad; and they seem to possess a greater significance than the memory of having chilblains or being unjustly accused of cribbing, the peculiar odiousness of a few of one's schoolfellows or the discomfort and danger of playing Post in a Ram.

There is not space here to speak of the Worshipful Company of Arch-Scugs or the reasons why Gathorne-Hardy minor threw an egg at the captain of the house. I was not in the division that bribed a tramp to sit with them during a Greek lesson, nor was I one of the three boys who went to see their tutor one Sunday morning and found a glass of milk and a slice of cake on a plate by his desk. One drank the milk, one ate the cake and the third broke the plate. Perhaps the story has no lesson to teach but for some reason it has always amused me. There is something stimulating about it. As I have said earlier, some masters had to endure a certain amount but on the whole they seemed to survive, more indeed than the boys, several of whom died in the course of the four or five years I was there, including one who used to sit next to me. Soon after my arrival a former head-master was buried at an advanced age. The Corps lined the streets. It was a wet day and a member of my house who was on duty in this rôle commissioned his fag to hold an umbrella over him during the ceremonial.

The Corps made up a whole battalion. It wore a heather-mixture uniform with light-blue piping and used to march along singing:

> 'When we go out we always shout
> We're bothered if we'll be bothered about,
> We won't be bothered about.'

It was officered by masters and supplied with an adjutant from the regular army. The adjutants were admirable men, and one, a miracle of smartness, used to appear suddenly from behind a pillar and give alarming shouts of '*Rip those faces away!*' I used to enjoy field-days and once a boy in my company shot an umpire in the neck with a date-stone fired from a rifle. Keenness on the Corps varied, however, and one house turned out for the house-section cup all wearing horn-rimmed spectacles and to the surprise of the Guardee, who had come down from the barracks

to judge the event, numbered off: 'one, two, three,
four, five, six, seven, eight, nine, ten — knave — queen
— king — ace.' After what seemed many years of long
service and good conduct I succeeded in becoming a
sergeant, in the teeth of my company-commander,
a master who had been almost entirely responsible
for winning the war but disliked me because I had
once warned him that the puttee on his left leg was
about to come down. At the end of each summer the
Corps went to camp.

There is no doubt that the most dramatic way to
leave Eton was to be expelled instantly and drive
away in the middle of the half. For the majority
there was this anti-climax of ten days under canvas
on Salisbury Plain. On my last morning at the
school I woke up feeling far from well. The excite-
ments of saying good-bye all round, having dinner with
m'Dame and helping to give a small informal party
with some other boys who were also leaving, had
proved too much. Something had disagreed with me.
It was an effort to get into uniform. Things came to a
head on parade, which took place at about six or
seven in the morning. We were telling off by platoons
and, not wishing to disturb the ceremonial by anything
untoward, I fell out and went to sit on the hard seat
outside the Orderly Room. The company was
inspected. I watched, feeling like hell. Then the
man who had won the war came to have a look at me.
It was a bitter moment. Someone, perhaps one of the
staff-sergeants, suggested a cab. The idea was brilliant.
The company advanced from the right in column-of-

route and joined on to the end of the company in front. The other companies followed. I brought up the rear, at the tail of the column, in an open victoria with my rifle between my knees and my equipment on the opposite seat. The cab was driven by a Hogarthian character called Jo Springbottom. We must have been an impressive sight, recalling one of the tableaux in the Lord Mayor's Show. We rattled over Barnes Pool Bridge and up Windsor Hill. The pinnacles, the turrets, the incomparable elm-trees were left behind. My schooldays were over. I paid off the cab and, more dead than alive, trailed along the platform. I found the compartment somehow, and my disappointed section, who had hoped that I had been left behind permanently. In the train someone, not myself, smoked a large German pipe with a tin lid and a white china bowl, round which the picture of a love-scene had been painted in bright colours.

THE NOTIONAL MANNER

[Winchester]

BY J. N. RICHARDS

I WRITE these few lines on Winchester straight from a
stiff dose of Mr. T. S. Eliot. Only too easily the per-
vasive influence of tradition oppresses me. It forms
a sort of carapace which protects me as much from
inward doubts as from enemies on the outside. Like a
child stuffing himself with sugared plums, I can summon before me a pageant of schooldays set in a rosy
Pickwickian light. Gothic stones rise in front of me, a
bell tolls to call me to evensong on a Sunday afternoon,
and I pace back and forth the length of Meads accom-
panied by the scholarly ghosts of previous generations.
Such phantasies leave no room for doubt that, in the
words of Sir Henry Newbolt, mine is 'the best school
of all'. They put me in a good humour with myself.
'One of the brainy ones', is a description which seems
to fit. The tie I wear of red blue and brown stripes is
something, I feel, to be complacent about. Not for
worlds would I exchange the noble melody of Dulce
Domum for Wykehamist, Wykehamist ra, ra, ra.
And as I write I regret the absence of an audience for
this nice display of my manners. I slip very easily
into this condition of inflated dignity. Not a vulgar
strutting dignity, but an infinitely more persuasive

sense of superiority, well-bred and impregnable to the envious attacks of inferiors. These and similar feelings are the peculiar heritage of a Wykehamist, and he must consciously, though with regret, put them aside if he wishes to be candid.

My first experiences may be rapidly passed over. For the first time I enjoyed the distinction of being called a man, and this at the age of thirteen. I discovered the attractions of the school shop and learnt to spend my money on ice-creams, banana mashes and sausages. I was free to ride a bicycle. In the Hall of my house was allotted to me a 'toys' consisting of a wooden slab to sit on, a wooden slab to write on, and a cupboard for my books. On either side it was partitioned from its neighbours. This corner of semi-privacy I accepted more gratefully than I would now the full-privacy of a bed-sitting room. But such satisfactions as these are of little interest. Every boy, I imagine, on becoming a Public School Man experiences them.

However, there is one particular initiation I cannot pass over. I refer to 'notions'. Every school has to a certain extent a language of its own. Holidays for example are referred to as hols, a disappointment is a swizz and so on. These terms are well-known and anyone who cared to take the trouble could easily compile a juvenile vocabulary for himself. But at Winchester our specialized dialect was of an altogether different order. The idioms which we used, peculiar to ourselves, were so numerous and elaborate as almost to constitute a separate language parallel and supplementary to the King's English. They were codified and set forth in a book called Winchester College Notions, the greater part of which every new boy was required to know by heart after the first fortnight, under penalty of a beating in case of failure. My own copy of this fascinating work I have unfortunately lost, so I am only able to quote such gems as remain in my memory. And 'prates' (pronounced pratees) is the word that comes first to my mind. It means potatoes. I remember that, taking my first meal in the school, I innocently inquired of the boy sitting next to me if he would mind passing the potatoes.

'We don't say that here,' he answered contemptuously, 'We say: "Prates please".'

In this way I received my first lesson in Winchester College notions and Wykehamical manners. Another interesting word is 'pitch-up'. This designates parents. If I had my dictionary by my side I could doubtless furnish a scholarly explanation of the origin of this term. Without it I like to think that the word refers back to the ejaculatory powers of child-birth, but that, in the process of time, the derivation being forgotten it has acquired the respectability of polite usage. This smoothing of rough edges, or softening of philological rudeness, which is wholly in the Wykehamical tradition, may be observed likewise in the word 'tart'. This is nothing to eat, nor is it a woman who sells her body. It means a favourite or popular boy. Thus a young man with good looks and a gracious manner might be a house tart, or with better fame and fortune, a school tart.

I might add indefinitely to the list. The letters
S.R.O.G.S. presented difficulties both of interpreta-
tion and pronunciation. I learnt that when I referred
to this society I must say 'Shrogus' and that these
letters stood for Shakespeare Reading and Orpheus
Glee Society. I was told never to say paper but
'bumph'. I was taught that a man was not clever, but
a jig; he was not good at French or mathematics, but
a French jig or a mathma jig. And our language was
as notable for its reticences as for its assertions. Thus
the holidays were neither 'holidays' nor 'hols', but a
vacation, and we used the word with conscious
superiority. But perhaps the best joke of all was
getting a 'pempe'. The unfortunate new boy was
asked by his examiner to get a 'pempe' from someone
in another House. If he was wise he smiled sheepishly
and took it as a joke. But if he was gullible and had
not learnt the secret of the comedy he set out on his
fruitless errand. The first boy he was sent to inquire of
referred him to another, and this other referred him to
a third and so on. And he was left to roll his Sisyphus'
stone until such time as the joke was held to have gone
far enough and become tedious. The reader will be
glad to know that I did not fall into this trap. In
other respects my experience was less satisfactory. At
the beginning of my second year it was my duty to
teach a new boy the notions I had learnt the year
before. He was a bright high-spirited creature and I
was altogether unable to impress upon him the serious
nature of our studies. Without actually saying so, he
plainly regarded this whole business as buncombe,

and when, after his first fortnight, he came to be examined, he was unable to satisfy the examiners. For this I was beaten.

Apart from the first flush of hope, I find, unless I look closely in my memory for better things, that the record of my schooldays is a record of humiliations. The humiliations I speak of were purely personal in character. I am not joining myself with those who are vexed at the Officers Training Corps. On the contrary, beyond a certain weariness of the spirit induced by the shining of buttons and the polishing of belts, or the continual reiteration of placing my rifle on my shoulder and then placing it on the ground again, according to the strict numbers of military etiquette, I can truthfully say that it had no effect upon me whatever. And I find it difficult to imagine what other effect these weekly exercises can possibly have on a normally intelligent boy. As for the field days, with the railway journey, the smoking, and the general good temper, they were a welcome relief from the monotony of regular school life. But on the whole I can safely dismiss the Winchester College O.T.C. as profoundly boring.

Nor, in an access of self-pity, can I arouse myself to any pitch of excitement over the squabble about standardization versus self-expression. I remember listening to a debate on this subject in the school debating society or Deba Sa as a good Wykehamist should express himself. One of the speakers suggested to his audience that the Public School system might be likened to a sausage-machine – all kinds of meats were put into it, but only a monotony of sausages came out at the other end. I laughed with the best of them at this chestnut, but I return to it in a serious frame of mind. It seems to me that in a world where standardization is the rule of life, where there is a progressive tendency towards a planned economy and a planned polity, it is the plain duty of our schools to fall into line with this tendency and to arrange the planning of our young men as early and efficiently as possible. Those few, the natural toughness of whose characters makes them impervious to this treatment, must be content to remain the misfits and the idle poor of the modern world.

But, in such short space, it is more congenial to expose my masters than myself. If I wished to compile a record of fatuity the richness of my material would embarrass me. School sermons, perhaps, offer as good a field as any for the researcher after pedagogic stupidity. There is one gem I cannot pass over. Here it is. 'God is like a camel walking through the desert dropping dung as he goes. We are that dung.' Nor can I forget those chatty little sermons of everyday life, the descriptions of his wife's cruise to the Holy Land ('when we came to Mount Sion my wife's hat blew off') with which another preacher used to instruct us.

But this is no better than gossip. And it is unfair. Boys are notoriously malicious and quick sighted to pierce the pretensions of their elders and betters. The character saintly enough to come unscathed through a year of school-mastering does not exist. Therefore, let me confine myself to those I knew best.

To begin with my form-master then. Though he taught me little, I was reasonably happy. He was a man of between fifty and sixty and more benevolent than otherwise. More than anyone I have met, I think he had caught the essential point of that sentiment which we refer to vaguely in such terms as 'the public school spirit', 'playing the game', 'the team spirit', etc. I do not believe he had a very profound interest in his work. When he was young he probably had but by the time I knew him it had largely evaporated and condensed again in two other directions, talking and gardening. As for talking, I am sure that it was only his sense of duty that the work must be got through that ever made him stop. In his garden, he was happy altering it and planning new arrangements. A path would be constructed and a junction christened, tulip-tree junction, perhaps. And he was hairless. I remember how agreeably surprised I was one morning when he vouchsafed us this information. Some boy, I think, had excused himself for being late by saying that the water had been cold for shaving. 'I don't have to shave because no more hairs come,' he replied.

Tall, thin, round faced and hairless, he was not, you will say, an impressive sort of man to control some thirty young boys. And yet between himself and his class there was perfect subconscious understanding. It was based on a mutual desire to be left alone. He on his part expected the necessary work to be performed, a reasonable standard of manners and good behaviour, and an audience to listen to his conversation. We on our part were all the more ready to listen because it meant that so much less time would be left for working. And we expected not to be overworked and not to be pressed into extraneous intellectual pursuits we were not interested in. On these terms we were an exceedingly well organized community. The work was done and nobody was put out. We made the best of our circumstances and no one's conscience had anything to be ashamed of. This is what I mean by saying that we were a perfect example of the public school spirit in action.

The happiness of our circumstances was brought home to me by a small breakdown in which I was involved. I had been set to write an essay, the subject of which I don't remember. I was told to come and see my form-master at a certain time to have it corrected. I forgot to come. I received a note appointing another time. I arrived late. When I got there he was standing with my essay in his hands. He looked at me, tore it in half and threw it into the waste-paper basket. 'That's what I think of your essay,' he said, and walked out of the room.

I realized that the equilibrium of life had been upset. He had come all the way from his house and I had not arrived. I had been the cause of wholly unnecessary inconvenience. And only a week before he had been happily telling us that he no longer shaved because no hairs came. I felt a horrible cad.

And now for my house-master. I have before me a diary which I kept at the time. For almost every day there is a reference to the 'Greaser' or the 'Oiler'.

This is how we spoke of him. I think we must have allowed outward appearances to lead us astray. Originally these terms must have arisen from the man's heavy black jowl and smooth voice, purely physical attributes. But imperceptibly they led us towards a judgment of character which I feel convinced was grossly unfair. This diary gives me much cause for regret. On one occasion, I see, I asked him what he thought of the character of Wackford Squeers. I am glad to say that this malicious impertinence left him quite unperturbed. Another entry refers to a certain lottery. I should explain that it was a frequent complaint of ours that we were not properly fed. We criticized in the usual way the system which threw the financial responsibility for the catering entirely on the house-masters' hands. Such criticisms school-boys very generally make and I am not saying that in this case they had any justification. Nevertheless complain we did, and the accepted reason for our supposed neglect was the continual growth of our House-master's family. Accordingly, in the expectation of a happy event, a lottery was organized with prizes for the winners according as a boy or a girl or twins were born. Now it is a curious thing that so far as I can recollect my House-master had no family at all neither when I went to school nor when I left. Yet so strong was the prevailing impression that he had that this lottery was organized, and to this day my money has not been returned to me. I repeat these things with shame and to make amends and I must acknowledge the smiling good humour with which he bore his boys' opinion of him, of which he was perfectly conscious.

To conclude these random reminiscences I should like to be able to lead to some guiding principle of education, but I can think of none. I have no axe to grind. I will only add a word of gratitude to Winchester that my education has admirably suited me to the life of leisure which I find most congenial to my temper.

POTTING SHED OF THE ENGLISH ROSE

[Sherborne]

BY E. ARNOT ROBERTSON

'RUN about, girls, *like* boys, and then you won't think *of* them.' That was Sherborne. Not that anything of the kind could ever be said openly, of course, because this would be to admit not only the existence of boys – horrid — but also that unless kept on the hop nice minded English girls in their teens occasionally speculated about them. Horrid with three stars, in the unwritten Baedeker of the Nasty which ruled our young lives. Almost every human activity seemed to be in it, except cricket. Cricket was compulsory at Sherborne.

It is nice to feel that no misfortune that happens to me — neither illness nor poverty, the most probable — can possibly make me quite as unhappy as I was at Sherborne; for the adult mind, when wretched, can find some compensations, however small, but the child's can't: and I would like to make clear at the beginning that I know I am being unjust to the school because I was unhappy there; presumably there must have been something good about it, for everyone was not as unhappy as I was. Indeed, lots of the girls ran about even more than they were required to do by a curriculum that made little allowance for time spent in getting from one place to another. (Hockey in the winter, also compulsory: run, girls, run!)

Perhaps the teaching was good. Certainly I can still remember, as one of the few relics of my education, that

'Common are to either sex
Artifex and opifex',

and something effective must have been done to impress this on my memory because I have no idea now what either of them means, and I doubt that I ever knew, not having an inquiring mind in this direction.

Anyway, it wasn't the food. I fancy I lived chiefly, at the age when I was growing fastest, on malt and codliver oil, which I was lucky in liking. This was an extra, so that one could have as much as one liked.

It is very difficult to convey the atmosphere of an English public school for girls to anyone who has the good fortune not to have been sent to one. They are — or at least this one was in my time — run on a male system imperfectly adapted to female needs. We were terribly, terribly keen on games. A carefully fostered and almost entirely spurious interest in house matches was our main subject of conversation. Girls at boarding school ages are suggestible almost beyond belief: trying to recall now the inter-girl talks that took place when authority was not in hearing, I remember snatches of discussion, in which we vied with one another in the single-minded animation expected of us, as to whether Wingfield's second eleven was likely to do better than last year against Aldhelmsted Juniors, these being two of the houses. Now I do not believe that sporting conjecture of this kind comes natural to one girl in twenty; but this was the tradition of the place (officially described as The High Moral Tone of the School) and so this was how we talked, even when alone.

Naturally the school rules laid down that one did not have to play games when one was not well, but the Sherborne spirit made other claims (run, girls, run: this is the first function of English womanhood, and never mind the later ones). Coddling oneself was two-stars horrid, and a form of shyness was inculcated, not intentionally but by the tradition, which made it difficult at match times to get out of playing. So one played. This was voluntary idiocy on the girls' part, but in that atmosphere it was an almost inevitable idiocy and should have been foreseen. Authority however, in my time, which was during and after the War, was lacking in imagination over health save in one curious respect. It was thought very important that girls should not be encouraged to become hypochondriacs, so that if one rather too often had a headache, or any of the reasonless malaises that affect perfectly healthy girls in the over-growing years, it was sometimes difficult to get permission to lie down because it was feared that one might be malingering. It is hard to imagine that any normal child would ask to lie down in a darkened room in the day-time for fun, or that if in some way abnor-

mal, and deprived of this pecular form of amusement,
could possibly be the better for being forced into some
sort of activity: but I can still remember clearly with
loathing every step of the way down to the Abbey and
back — about a mile — on a Sunday morning when I
had a bilious attack and wanted to go to bed; and the
look of the windy playing field on which I unwillingly
watched a hockey match with violent neuralgia
on a winter afternoon. On both occasions I had
asked permission to stay in, but my temperature had
been taken and as this was normal and I could therefore be assumed free from infectious illness, about
which infinite precautions were taken, I had no
adequate excuse. Hardy as well as sporting, that was
the Sherborne Type, of which we heard a great deal.
I was frequently asked whether I did not want to
be it — a rhetorical question which I never had the
moral courage to answer truthfully.

If you have a daughter at a public school, which
heaven or sensible parenthood forbid, you will have
seen a reassuring paragraph in the prospectus which
reads in all cases something like 'Great and
individual care is taken of the girls' health'.
Imagine for yourself the difficulty of taking great or
individual care of the health of two or three hundred
girls in a lump, while encouraging that lump to be as
refinedly boyish as possible; and I have never
heard of any girls' public school that was not a
weak copy of a boys'.

That paragraph usually goes on something about
'remedial exercises . . . best modern methods . . .

under competent supervision of trained medical staff. . . .' This means walking about the gym on tiptoe for a quarter of an hour as a cure for flat feet on days when the junior games mistress can be spared to conduct the performance. In my case, as I had not got flat feet, it was probably considered a cure for being a minor nuisance: the one thing in which the school and I saw eye to eye was that I was not the best raw material for the Sherborne Type. The head-mistress once told me in an expansive moment that she had prayed about me more than about any girl then under her care. The failure of these inter-cessions to 'take' on me satisfactorily was one of the first things to shake my belief in the efficacy of prayer.

This early loss of faith made Sunday in term time a more trying day for me than it would have been anyway. While we were dressing a bell rang for five minutes silence in which we were required to pray or read the Bible. Then came House Prayers, down-stairs. After breakfast the walk to the Abbey, morning service, the walk back, and then lunch. Scripture preparation for week-day Bible lessons came before tea, and evening service afterwards. Finally House Prayers followed supper and then we had five minutes more Silence for private religious indulgence of some kind before Lights Out. Sunday evening ended officially with the singing of the School Hymn which started 'Now our day of rest is over.'

One of the few promises I made to myself in child-hood which I have been able to keep (most of them were on a huge scale and included being beautiful, famous, and witty, or alternatively the lover, though not specifically the mistress, of a king, if any could be found worthy) was that when I was free I would never go into a church again save for sightseeing or the weddings of other people.

However, it is only fair to the school (not that I could be, after so much unhappiness there) to add that several of my contemporaries got religion; and two, I believe, have become missionaries.

There would have been much grief and nagging, from the other girls and not only from the staff and prefects, if it had ever been discovered that I used the five minutes' silence, morning and evening, to finish off preparation which I could never manage to get through in the allotted hours, by smuggling up school books in the legs of my knickers. Public opinion would have been horrified not because this might pull me ahead in work — I could never do more than just not disgrace the House in this line — but because it was supposed to break one's School Honour to disregard a rule. Everything affected one's 'honour', the hardest worked word in our narrow world. And if one broke a rule one was expected to confess it to a prefect and have a nice spiritual wallow together. Other girls did, too, but as my honour was never intact for more than a day or so at a time I felt that this was not worth while. This system produced the most thorough going prigs imaginable. At my first, smaller, healthy minded school we all smuggled in sweets whenever we could: at Sherborne when I managed to bring some back one term everyone refused them smugly because they were against the rules, and I was forced by public opinion to give them up to authority.

The point that I want to make with simple and, I hope, disarming conceit is that if I were a hopeless misfit from the start it may not have been altogether my fault, because I was an extremely ordinary child in every way; or every way but one. Indeed, if there could have been competitions in ordinariness, I should have come out high, being more ordinary than most, only much less suggestible: this was the snag. The slightly hysterical atmosphere of 'Oh-goody-goody-we-ought-to-do-well-in-lacrosse-this-term. Hurrah-for-the-house-and-I'm-so-glad-I'm-not-pretty,' fostered no seeds of enthusiasm in my mind. And without that enthusiasm, vague but ready for anything that could reflect credit on the House, life at Sherborne was either one long pretence or one long nag. The School Type, which was our pattern, was the epitome of the team spirit. And this spirit, like prolonged discussion of sport, just does not come naturally to the female. Why should it? Unlike the male, whose primitive functions include collective hunting, she has no instincts which it can serve. In fact, given the least encouragement, her instincts will make the team spirit impossible. I still feel that I was instinctively sound in regarding the House as a collection of thirty affectedly boyish little girls and nothing more. At intervals I said so, which was not so sound, and explains, if any explanation is needed, why I was extremely unpopular, which also explains some of my

feeling that going to this school is the worst thing that
has happened to me. But it is not the whole·explan-
ation. After I left it took me two or three years to get
over my schooldays in health. (I can never remember
being without a heavy cold there in the winter—why,
oh why are almost all institutions run by women so
appalling as to draughts and food? This criticism is
general and not particular.) And it took me much
longer than that to get over the horrible feeling with
which we were subtly inoculated about sex — that it
was something so beastly lying in wait for us that we
were not to think about it (run, girls, run.) On the
other hand it was made very difficult to forget because
of the frequent references to purity. I remember the
headmistress — not the present one, under whom
everything is a lot better, I am told — telling us in
an emotional address that she trusted us alone in the
bathrooms. What she trusted us about I had at the
time no idea.

The use of physical force not being favoured in girls'
schools, I got away with my observations about the
House with a whole skin, but that was about all that
did come undamaged through this expensive potting
shed of the English rose. I have two recurrent night-
mares from which I suffer at about six months'
intervals, and probably always shall: one is the usual
dream experience of falling and waking just before the
crash, which is terrifying, but the other is much
worse: I am going back to Sherborne, starting all
over again, and there is no chance of escape. Inside
I am exactly what I am to-day, married and an author

and so on, but I cannot convince anyone of this because I cannot remember the names of my books, everyone assures me that there is no such man as my husband, and outwardly I am exactly what I was at fifteen. I generally wake up sweating with fright. Goodness knows, supposing that nowadays I had to spend twelve or thirteen weeks shut up with thirty women of my own age I should be appalled at the job of choosing them: I can only think of about six of whom I could stand such a heavy dose. But the companionship of that number of chance-picked girls at the dullest ages, when the body is growing too fast to leave surplus energy for the mind, was made no pleasanter by the fact that as a companion I was as dull as any of them. The remark 'I'm glad I'm not pretty,' quoted before and made by a member of my house who certainly had much to be thankful for, reflects equally well the general level of our intelligence and the feeling about sex in the school.

There were other girls who loathed the place as I did, but they always prevailed on their parents to let them leave so that I lost my potential friends. I was handicapped by having a cousin who was the perfect example of the Type into which we were all supposed to be compressed. Bright and enthusiastic about almost everything by nature, she revelled in Stiff-Upper-Lippery, sending back glowing reports of jolly Sixth Form doings, while I, a squidgy part of Upper Four (b), wrote home monotonous and incoherent complaints, trying vainly to convey, with the vocabulary of fifteen or sixteen years old, that it was not any specific thing I hated but all that the school stood for. (As I have said, this was during and just after the War, and as since then the whole staff has changed, presumably everything else has changed too except the school buildings. They were all right.)

If only I had had the sense to stick to describing the food, meal by meal, I might have got away earlier. As it was, my parents felt, not unnaturally, that my cousin's detailed account of topping work and ripping play was more convincing than my inarticulate woes, and it was felt that what was called 'the rough and tumble of school life' would rub off my corners. There wasn't any rough and tumble, which I should by then have fiercely enjoyed as an outlet, only a monotony of semi-male impersonation, which was beyond a child's powers of description; and starting spiritually in the round, so to speak, I developed more corners than anyone could have had without the help of the team spirit.

Release came eventually through my happy decision not to be confirmed when the time came. My reason for this was no more profound than that of the unwisely handled mule when it refuses to budge in any direction: 'they' wanted it, so there must be a catch somewhere. My loss of faith would not have been sufficient reason for letting myself be nagged at by the unfortunate prefects, who were set on to walking round the grounds with me after lunch on Sunday to try to persuade me. They felt just as shy about religion as I did. I was in the morbid stage of youthful apostasy when I alternately disbelieved in all heavenly powers and then felt sure that I was eternally damned for my disbelief.

Walking round with prefects for acutely self-conscious but supposedly helpful little talks was another of the features of our day of rest. I could find no reason for my continued refusal. They, poor conscientious girls, could find very few reasons to advance in favour of confirmation, except that the preparation classes were 'simply topping'; but then so, I had been given to understand, was compulsory cricket, and I knew all about that. They were agonizing walks.

Eventually, in desperation, one of the prefects asked me whether I did not think religion 'so sensible', and suddenly this crystallized Sherborne for me. A place where a collection of incredible legends — among them, in the New Testament, the most moving and lovely human story I had heard — could be described as 'so sensible'. I started writing home letters that were no longer plaintive but threatening: either I was taken away or I would do something desperate to get myself expelled, which would not be difficult in my case: I had recently got out on to the bathroom roof and danced a jig, so that my honour was bankrupt again: they could choose. My cousin had left, so I won.

I sat up, hunched on a corner of my bed, all my last night at Sherborne, unwilling to waste in sleep a moment of gloating over the fact that my public school life was over: the official end of my childhood had come: how exquisitely delightful it would be to be an adult! And it is: the state of not being a child

163

has surpassed even my expectations of joy. The simple pleasure that I take in this is the best thing my education gave me; apart, of course, from the cultural value of knowing the hermaphroditic qualities of artifex and opifex, whatever they are.

DAY BOY

[University College School]

BY STEPHEN SPENDER

I CONSIDER myself very lucky in having been educated at U.C.S. Above all else, because it was a day school.

I contrast it sharply in memory with my preparatory boarding schools. When I was nine, I was sent to a preparatory school. This was during the War. At the end of the hall of this school there was a platform and under that platform there was a hole, where, for some reason the remnants of the day's food were always put, so that it was called the 'Bloater Hole'. For four terms, I was unceasingly shoved down the 'Bloater Hole' by other boys. One day, I and a few other boys, being hungry during the 'break', ate four quarters of a slice of bread, instead of only a quarter, as we were allowed to. This was discovered. The house-master assembled all the boys, and standing on the platform (above the 'Bloater Hole'), said words to this effect: 'These boys are worse than huns, they're FOOD HOGS. I'm not going to try and discover the culprits. I leave it to the remainder of you to do what you like with them. I outlaw them.' We were soon discovered. Some boys tied pieces of rope round my arms and legs and pulled in different directions.

It so happened that immediately after the incident I was to have a music lesson. The music master was called Greatorex, a man whom all the boys loved. I could not play the piano, and I burst into tears. He asked me very gently what was the matter. I told him, and he said, 'You may go on being unhappy until you are twenty or so, and a year comes when you are very free and only waiting to go up to the University. You will probably travel abroad and then that will perhaps be the happiest time of your life.' In the completest sense, I understood what he meant. I think that I shall be grateful to him all my life for having told me that one got happy when one was older. Everyone else used to say, 'How I wish I was young. How happy one is when one is a boy.'

My father, realizing that all was not well with me, took me away from this school, just as I was getting used to it, and sent me to another that was far worse. I never told him I did not like it, as each school seemed to be more horrible than the last. This school was run in the most dishonest way. For example, one summer term the amazed but sceptical boys returned from their homes to discover that it was quite trans-formed. The head master's drawing-room had been turned into a boys' study. There was a tennis court. The boys had gardens. I, as the son of a literary man, was appointed school librarian. The next term, as suddenly all these benefits had evaporated, and we lived in the old way, cooped up in a minute changing room and made to play in a back yard of asphalt. But a lovely photogravure school prospectus had been published with captions such as 'Boys playing tennis'. 'What book, please?' 'The boys' study'. 'Gardening', etc., under the photographs.

The head master loved caning. One Sunday, after he had come home from a game of golf, he caned my brother for kicking a tennis ball about the class-room.

At this school something far worse happened to me than the Food Hog incident. It was intensified by the fact that it involved my brother as well. One dreadful day the boys discovered that our mother's name was Schuster. After that they always called, and treated us, as 'Huns'. A boy would come up to me and tell me that my brother Humphrey had spat or grunted in a Teutonic manner, thus giving away the family secret. He would tell Humphrey the same about me, and often they would play us against each other when we were together. In this way they succeeded in turning our love into a feeling of frightened and hysterical rivalry, in which each tried to prove that he had not betrayed the other, and this sometimes flared up into hatred.

One day I came to realize that the person I should attack was not my brother, but the ringleader of the boys who were persecuting us. I therefore challenged him to a fight. I do not remember who won, but I do remember that while we were fighting a small and cowardly boy called Wallace, whom I had often protected, sneered at me and shouted, 'Yah, Hun!' When we had finished fighting I addressed myself to him. I remember him looking very terrified and I remember that he was leaning against the closed window. I raised my arm, and I do not remember whether I struck him, but I must have looked cruel. He fell back against the window, which was smashed, although he was not hurt. There was an awed exuberant fall of silence on the boys in the changing room as they looked forward to the prodigious punishment that would doubtless fall on me.

Just then the mistress came into the room in order to fetch us for our walk. She immediately saw what had happened and she went to tell the head master. She came back and told me I was requested not to go on the walk with the other boys. After two hours the troop returned, full of speculation about my fate. We then had to go into the classroom for chapel with the head master. When he saw me, he said in a trembling voice: 'You are not good enough to pray with the other boys. Go away.' I went.

Nothing happened that night, except that I could not sleep, and with a return of tenderness that seemed more than ever to make us foreigners and to take us home, my brother held my hand very tightly. In the morning, I was allowed to go into school. A feeling of joy began to rise in me: I felt that perhaps my outrage was so fearful that it was entirely beyond punishment. But no. I was sent for during the second lesson of the day. The head master stood in his study and looking at me in what appeared to me to be a very penetrating way, said: 'You are a boy, who for a long time has puzzled me. I think now I understand you. Bend over.' He caned me, and then shook my hand.

I have digressed thus far because my whole attitude

to U.C.S. was influenced by these experiences. When I entered this gentlest of schools, I was like all the other boys from the preparatory school, sadistic. We had, of course, deeply and instinctively realized that the head master was sadistic. It would have surprised my parents to have known that they might just as well have had me educated at a brothel for flagellants as at the school referred to, but it was so, and I am sure it is equally true of many other preparatory schools.

Secondly, I arrived at U.C.S. in terror of ever again being 'understood' in the sense in which my other head master had said he understood me. I was always imagining that people were seeing through me and that what they saw was very little indeed.

However, Guy Kendall, the head master, interviewed me and gave me such high marks for this interview that I started work in the fourth form. I soon settled down and I did not find the work too hard. The boys were friendly, and in all the time I was at that school I never heard of any case of bullying. One or two of the boys were naturally ill-disposed, but the feeling of the boys was influenced by the gentle spirit of the head master and most of the staff.

What I enjoyed most at U.C.S. was the social life. There were any number of societies, the chief of which was the debating society. I used to go to all the Debates, and I used to speak, very unsurely, from notes. My strong subjects were the League of Nations and Free Trade. Free Trade, I could enter into most fully, but there were points at which the League of Nations became History or Geography and here my feeling that I could never learn or understand anything, completely destroyed my interest. I remember being particularly depressed at my complete inability to *think*. For I had very purist conceptions. I imagined constructive thought as being completely independent of any sense-perceptions, and therefore quite without content. Yet it did not occur to me that this was impossible. I merely believed that when people talked about thinking they meant this, and I therefore knew that to me it was impossible to think. I thought of work in the same way, as being void, tireless, unrewarding industry. The moment anything interested me, I could not think of it as work, so I gave myself no credit for it: indeed I regarded it as 'easy' which was the opposite of 'work' and therefore a vice almost. My inhibition even applied to difficult games. From hearing people boast of their skill I concluded there must be something difficult in games and that therefore I could not play them: not because I was afraid but because I could not apprehend the nature of the difficulty which I was expected to overcome. I was thus surrounded by impossibilities. And I think this led me naturally to poetry, because poetry was the means of expression which was completely possible to me, and which in no sense involved my proving that I was better able to do things than other people, but consisted in my being singularly myself and not other people.

Amongst other things I am grateful to U.C.S. for teaching me to understand the lives of those who were poorer than myself. I was brought up by my parents to regard a certain standard of living as being supremely important in life. When I was a child I was never allowed to play with poor children because my mother regarded them as not only rough, but also as perpetual carriers of infectious diseases. When I was at my preparatory school I compared myself with the other boys, most of whom were sons of shopkeepers, and I decided that the difference between them and myself must be that I was an aristocrat: I believed this so spontaneously that the boys accepted it from me without dispute. I once learned that one of the masters lived in a bed-sitting-room and I was overwhelmed with horror at my first contact with the truly sordid.

However, when I had been at U.C.S. for several terms, I accidentally discovered that twenty-five per cent. of the boys were scholars from L.C.C. schools. I made tactful inquiries, and I soon realized that some of the boys whom I most liked were of working-class parents and lived in very poor districts. This taught me two things. Firstly, to a large extent it explained to me the gentleness of U.C.S. For the sons of the wealthy and finely bred in England are often dominated by a certain harsh exclusiveness. In the ordinary public school most of the boys are intensely competitive, to a degree which is not only accounted for by the system: each boy is an earnest little propagandist for his own vices or virtues, his excellences at games, his badness at work, his lack of interest in the arts, etc., and the boys are only united in maintaining a kind of pact by which any boy who shows genuine distinction of character or originality of mind will be persecuted. But working-class boys are not jealous in the same way. They are amused at the eccentricities of each other, without being cruelly malicious, and they have a quite extraordinary respect for excellence of any kind. At the end of my time at U.C.S. when I was on the library committee, and was an editor of the school magazine, and a sub-monitor, my opinions seemed to be taken quite seriously and I had no enemies. As soon as I got to Oxford, I found myself surrounded by public school boys who sneered at me because I was an aesthete, were indignant because I was a 'red', and who on one occasion tried to break up my rooms. For this reason I felt far freer at U.C.S. than I ever did in the snobbish environment of Oxford.

Secondly, from watching the scholarship boys, I learnt that the standard of living in our house was absurd. Until I was sixteen, my father gave me six-pence a week pocket money (which then rose to 1/-), we were scarcely ever allowed to go to theatres or cinemas, and we were always being told to economize. Yet I realized that I belonged to one of the richest families of the school. I soon noticed that other boys whose parents had incomes of perhaps £500 a year, lived much jollier lives; they went to skating rinks, cheap theatres and cinemas; with the family they rattled about the countryside in old and tinny motor cars. Yet we lived at the rate of about £2000 a year (I do not know the exact figure) and we were not allowed to enjoy ourselves. All our money went on expensive doctors, nurses, companions, servants and high class food. We lived in a house that was too large for us, and on Sundays we went, dressed in 'Etons' to a large congregational church.

The chief problem of a day school is the balance in the life of each boy between his life at home and at school. There were some boys at U.C.S. whose home life interfered with their life at school: they were perhaps prevented from going to school by their parents. One boy was 'taken up' by an Anglo-Catholic priest, and was often away for whole days so that he might attend special Masses, or meet the Bishop of London. But such interference was rare, and, on the whole, I believe it was a good thing for most of us that we were half the day at home. The boy at boarding school, being away from home eight or nine months in the year, often does not have the slightest idea what his parents are really like. If he is neurotic he may, when it is too late, have to waste years trying to find out facts about his earliest environment, which are the first realities which it is natural for people to face.

My own home life was a painful but necessary experience which profoundly modified the happiness of my life at school. My mother had died when I was twelve years old, and my father, who was forty-five years older than my eldest brother, was overwhelmed by the sense of his responsibility towards us. He understood us well when we were extremely young, but, as we grew up, he regarded us with suspicion and horror. The way in which he loved us became a disease of anxiety. His only principle in taking care of us seemed to be, to prevent us from in any way growing up; and this struggle caused suffering on both sides, especially, as I now realize, on his.

Once, when we were on a holiday at the seaside, I remember watching my father lie in a hammock at the end of the garden. The harbour was below us. It was a perfectly calm day and in a little boat, which my father always watched, my eldest brother was sailing. My father did not speak, but, so great was his anxiety, that perspiration was pouring down his face. On another occasion, when I was sixteen, I tried to win back his long-lost faith in me, by telling him about some books that I was reading. I told him that I had just read a book by Bernard Shaw. My father stopped still in the path where we were walking and said: 'I have heard of other people having children like that, but I have always prayed God I might be spared.'

As I have said, we were only allowed sixpence a week pocket money, so that if ever we went out of the house and wished to take a 'bus ride, we had to go to my father and ask for leave; then he would either give us the necessary money, or he would go out with us himself, or he would send one of two faithful sisters who were servants and companions, out with us. During term we were not supposed to go to any amusements, and we lived under what my father lightly called 'a rigorous no-treat regime'. My father liked to use rather military language, and if one of us asked him for any favour, he would look elaborately sly, and say, 'Ah, I see that you're trying to get round my flank.'

What emerged more and more clearly from my home life was that our family was made different from the families of other boys by the extraordinary amount of fuss with which we were surrounded. My father had also somehow a *public* air which made him different from other parents. All his actions and sayings seemed to protest that they were important. He told long stories about Lloyd George. When he addressed one, he never spoke as a single man to a single boy. The whole vista of public life; the Liberal Party, Elections, the House, H.H.A., L.G. (as they were called), hung from his words. My father even addressed himself by his initials: he would relate to us how in moments of crisis he had said, 'Keep cool, H.S.', or 'Now H.S., don't lose your head'. I hated and feared these stories the more because I found a tendency towards the same kind of dramatization in myself; and, indeed, it is there now.

My father never punished us. But on one occasion, when I had forgotten to tell the servants that he was coming home for a certain meal, and no meal was prepared, he so impressed on me that my selfish indifference to him had violated the whole world of his life, that I was practically reduced to hysteria for the rest of the day. At such times, though, he suffered as violently as I did myself. The servants have told me how, if we wept for any reason, they would go into his study later and find him also weeping.

The revenge we took on him was never to laugh at his stories. At meals we would listen acidly to his conversation about politics, and if ever we could detect any inaccuracy in what he said, we would hasten to correct it. As he told the same stories many times, it was easy to upset him by pointing out how essentially the versions differed.

We lived in Frognal, within two minutes' walk of U.C.S., which is in the same road. The most dreaded of experiences was the daily bristly kiss which my father publicly planted on my face each morning at ten minutes to nine, at our garden gate and in front of a long procession of boys who trailed up to school. In order to avoid the full disgrace of this I took to going very early to school. I found I was happier there than at home, so I also would stay as long there in the evening as was possible.

One day a crisis was reached. At nine o'clock my sister and I were supposed to be in bed: we were working for Matric. — an examination which lay waiting for us, somewhere prepared like a sacrificial meal — so, out of respect for my father's wishes, we used to get up at six o'clock each morning and start working again. But on this occasion we were discovered working in the evening after nine. My father made a scene, and sent us to bed. By a process of logic familiar to him, but which I could never understand, the next morning whilst I was at school, he came suddenly into the classroom where I was working, and said to the Mathematics master, 'You must make my son Stephen work harder.'

I was considerably upset, and the boys all laughed. Their amusement proved to be my salvation. My best friend, a boy called Cornforth, immediately said that my father should be known as 'The Man of Wrath'. At first I was hurt, but soon I started to feel amused, and I told Cornforth about my life at home, and this relieved me considerably. Cornforth and one or two other boys used then quite often to invite me to their homes. I began to realize that through the companionship of these boys I could create the entirely personal humorous intimacy in my surroundings which I so needed. My life became intoxicated with companionship, and I wrote about my friends and would lie awake thinking of my happiness with them.

Although they were platonic, these friendships marked the end of adolescence for me. To some degree they released me even from physical inhibitions. My father had, of course, never discussed sexual matters with me, or even mentioned that sex existed. I became so afraid of coarse talk that I used to walk out of the room if I ever heard any of the boys using it. I was physically afraid of my own appearance. When I was a young boy I had quite enjoyed games, but a number of causes prevented me from doing so at U.C.S. One of these was my fear of being seen running about the field in shorts. Sometimes, especially if I were in uniform, it was a torture even to walk through the streets. I seemed to walk jerkily, and I stooped, and I was too tall for my age, and if it was winter I felt coldness like a mask cover my face and hands. Worst of all, it became impossible for me to use the lavatory during the eleven o'clock break, when all the other boys went to relieve themselves: the lack of concealment in such an act was an inconsistency that I could not understand, since I had learned to think that the whole of civilization was based on the concealment of physical acts. I was obliged either to wait for the lunch hour, when few people were about, or else to excuse myself from class. At the same time, my secret thoughts were extraordinarily debauched, and were quite unrelated to my manner of living.

My father died whilst I was still at school, and after his death I had a very happy last year. I have no doubt that it was only the conflict which was going on at home that prevented the other years from being as happy. I am grateful to U.C.S. for the gentleness and friendship it offered me: allowing me almost to educate myself and to cure myself of unnecessary unhappiness by the use of reason.

INDIAN INNOCENCE, LTD.

[Malvern]

BY DEREK VERSCHOYLE

I laugh off Spleen and keep my pence
From spoiling Indian innocence.
Matthew Green, 1734

FOR the enquirer behind the superficies of English
social life, nothing could be more enlightening than a
study of the prospectuses and periodical literature
produced by and on behalf of the English Public
Schools. What a paralysing uniformity one finds
displayed: in each pamphlet the same complacent
platitudes affirmed, the same principles adumbrated,
the same reassuring traditions invoked. They might
all have been turned out by the gross by the same
advertising agency. It is almost with pleasure, among
the slightly grotesque dummies mustered on parade
('The school prides itself on its record in athletics',
'Religious instruction forms a definite part of the
curriculum', 'Plain but wholesome food', 'There is a
flourishing O.T.C.') that one catches sight of a
generally anonymous villain: 'The school specializes
in the preparation of boys for the I.C.S. and the
Colonial Services.' Deceptively localized (this

particular statement does not issue from Malvern), the statement betrays upon reflection an affinity between the two systems that is too general to have been merely casually determined. It would be interesting if some social critic with full knowledge of the underworlds of education and Imperial politics in the eighteenth and nineteenth centuries would plot the graph of cause and effect that unites the two systems, and show, in particular, to what degree the relationship of master and pupil in the English Public Schools has been conditioned by the Colonial and Imperial policies of England during the last two hundred years. It is unnecessary at this date to enlarge on the exclusively restrictive nature of those policies until fairly recently. In a word, the operative principle has been to encircle the subjected native with the maximum amount of restriction compatible with leaving the burden of providing for physical survival himself. Announcements were periodically made that when the native had fully accepted the restrictions, dictated to him, when he had absorbed and grown to act in the light of the principles that determined them, when, in short, he had abandoned his own culture and adopted the alien mode of life imposed on him, some of the prohibitions would be relaxed. And, to give the credit due, some of them ultimately were.

This policy is closely paralleled in that process of juvenile enlightenment which, by an odd turn of phrase, has come to be known as the English Public School System. In the Public Schools the means of subsistence (theoretically, at any rate) are provided

by authority, and authority has thereby the wider
scope to impose restrictions. They are enforced (more
minutely than they can be on the Indian) in every
circumstance of school life. Physique, intellect and
religion are cultivated in the light of a prescribed
formula. Every member of the school is officially an
athlete, officially a student within a defined curriculum at the end of which lies an assigned examination,
officially (with few exceptions) a practising member
of the Church of England, officially a believer in and
a wielder of arms. Each activity is tinctured with a
creed of violence (who does not remember the reactionary bias of history text-books, the smug evasions
of preachers in the school chapel, the reasons for which
athletics were praised on speech-day platforms?). In
place of the Indian's genetic culture, the Public
Schoolboy abandons or suppresses the normal im-
pulses and energies of childhood. Actions, thoughts
and beliefs (and after the preliminary conditioning,
feelings) are standardized to the requirements of the
market. He is provided with newspapers which will
influence him 'safely' or not at all; *The Morning Post* to
cultivate the required opinions, *Punch* to add to his class-
consciousness and tether him, even in his view of what
is funny, to prevailing social codes, the usual picture
papers to warp any sense of cultural or literary
decency. Carefully chosen lecturers lend to the same
opinions the authority which the written word cannot
be relied upon to convey. There are few things more
instructive than to see the members of a Public School
attending a lecture. Row behind row, their faces

bowed in polite inattention, they sit in the school hall, occasionally lifting their heads to listen more closely while the eminent man on the platform describes some exciting incident on the Afghan frontier. Their expressions are as standardized as the sentiments in the school prospectus. The eloquence continues, and the eminent man builds up his little temple of orthodoxy. Each member of the audience, as he listens, comes one stage nearer to being that finished product, the Public Schoolboy. It does not matter that he is a standardized commodity, for that is what the market he has been produced for wants; a model of impersonal orthodoxy, from which personal determination has been eliminated. It is the manufacturer's mark that counts.

The most effective instrument in this process of elimination is traditionally that of fagging. When one considers the principles on which it is officially justified, it is not remarkable that the fagging system should have been devised not to cultivate a sense of responsibility and service in the boys who are liable to it, but to discourage it. For any boy of normal intelligence, sensitiveness and energy there can be nothing more depressive from effort than a system which enforces on him the performance of a number of tasks, bringing no pleasure or benefit to the performer or to the community in which he lives, to spare the pains of a senior boy for whom he has no reason to entertain any feeling other than hostility. No doubt public protest would have ended the system long ago, if any considerable percentage of boys had in the past left school while still at the fag-stage. The fact that this has not happened and the adaptability of boys of that age have insured the life of the system. As his critical faculties atrophy under a discipline that he cannot avoid, the boy becomes acclimatized to the system. By the time that his seniority has freed him from fagging, his sense of 'compensation' makes him approve of it. By this process the Public Schools secure the approbation of their products for the system. Having been a fag, the boy emancipated after three years' fagging agrees, he is the better able to sustain the authority of a prefect and order the conduct of a later generation of fags. (Correspondingly, having suffered as a fag the indignities and restrictions of an Indian native, he will thereby be enabled in later life as an administrator to compensate himself by enforcing official restrictions on the native. The Public Schools and Imperial policy are agreed on the rectitude of the code of an eye for an eye.)

It must be said of the system that it works effectively. I know of very few boys who left Malvern unconvinced of its virtues. There is no doubt a wide range of variation in the systems permitted in different schools, but I have no reason to believe that the one there enforced was less pointless than any other, or that some of its features are exceeded in barbarity in other schools. In my house any boy of less than three years' seniority who had not acquired immunity by reaching a certain form in the school, or a certain degree of athletic prominence, was liable to fag for any prefect who might want him at any hour of the day when he was not in his class-room.[1] The prefects' room was placed at the junction of two passages, on both sides of which were the boys' studies. When a prefect wanted anything done he would stand in the doorway of the prefects' room and bellow. At this signal anyone who was not immune from fagging had to rush towards the sound. The last to arrive (unless the prefect decided that he would prefer someone else, and it sometimes happened that the prefects agreed among themselves that an individual should be made to fag as much as possible) had to do whatever was required; it might be to run upstairs to save him the trouble of going to get a handkerchief for himself, it might mean walking a mile or so in the rain with notes for other prefects in perhaps half a dozen other houses. Sometimes a prefect shouted for a fag from another part of the house at the same time as there was a call from the prefects' room, and the spectacle of fags scattering to obey the conflicting calls of duty was considered very diverting by the by-standers. Those whose studies were furthest away from the prefects' room naturally arrived there last most frequently, and the ill-fated denizens of those distant hovels had a busy life. As well as casual

[1] Sometimes it happened that a particularly unfortunate or backward boy thus had to fag for someone of the same age as himself and with only a single term's seniority: an arrangement bad for both of them. Prefects were not appointed solely on account of their position in class. I remember that most of my 'leisure' during my first term at school was absorbed in doing the work of three prefects in my house who happened to be in the same form as I was. The work itself was simple; the difficulty lay in explaining how it was done to my task-masters. The least intelligent of them frequently acquired impositions, and these I had to do for him too. I should perhaps state, to anticipate a charge of malice, that I only had to fag for the minimum period of a year; and also, that I later became a prefect.

fagging, there were certain routine-duties whose performance fell to fags. These at least had the merit of
providing one half-hour in the day during which
prefects' calls for assistance could be disregarded
without recrimination. Few of them were other than
unnecessary and unpleasant, and some of them were
unrelievedly barbarous.[1] Generally each prefect had
the responsibility of detailing fags for one of these
occupations, and the opportunities thereby provided
for favouritism and the victimization of a boy by a
sadistic senior were considerable. But unpleasant as
they were, I think that the effect of these occupations
was considerably less injurious than that produced by
the ordinary course of casual fagging. There is a
world of difference between the effects of a settled
occupation, however humiliating, which has to be
performed at a known time, and the consequences of
waiting in one's study knowing that one may be called
upon to do something at any moment. This side of the

---

[1] As an example of barbarity, I will only mention the task of making toast
for the prefects. Two flaring and guttering gas-toasters were kept in an ill-lit
den under the staircase. On these machines the toast had to be made.
Toasting-forks were not permitted, and the toast had to be held in place
with the fingers. There were generally about eight boys struggling for
positions at the toasters, in a space barely adequate for three. As a result one
generally got pushed on to the machines, and burned both the toast and one's
hands. In winter chilblains always resulted from this activity, and as soon as
one got a chilblain one inevitably acquired a burn on top of it. It was a
perilous occupation, in which failure was rewarded with a beating. I assume,
though I have no evidence on the point, that some more humane procedure
will have been introduced by now.

As an example of futility, there was the polishing of brasswork on prefects'
O.T.C. uniforms and equipment. At one period it was rare for a Wednesday
(the day on which the O.T.C. paraded) to pass without some fag getting
thrashed for insufficient or untidy polishing. It apparently occurred to no
one that black buttons could have been substituted for brass without an
appreciable lowering of military discipline.

system was a direct invitation to, and general cause of idleness. The weaker in character among prefects were barely able to perform the most intimate bodily functions for themselves, and the corridors at certain hours of the day were just a continuous echo of calls for fags. As a result very few boys thought it worth their time to start doing anything of value or interest, when they were liable at any moment to have to chase down the passage and be sent on some trivial errand. I can remember finding groups of boys sitting in their studies, wasting time in the ordinary type of intermittent and allusive gossip, or even doing nothing but listen for a prefect's shout, hoping that by being ready they would avoid being the last to reach the prefects' room. A glimpse of those studies would have pleased Lord Baden-Powell. 'Be Prepared' was inscribed on every nerve. Work suffered of course, because one could only be certain of not being interrupted in the protective hour of official Preparation. It did much to perpetuate the barely infantile standards that prevailed in the lowest forms, and to form the magazine-habit[1] in the place of reading books.

But the enforcement of fagging is only one detail in the Public Schools' general anxiety to remove any opportunity for personal freedom. For the existence of this anxiety one has the further evidence of the

[1] In my house the magazine-habit had a strong ally in the quality of the books that were available in the house-library: the dullest of insignicant fiction (Zane Grey to about the Buchan level), books of 'adventure', the autobiographies of reactionary politicians and public men, costume-history by 'safe' writers. One's own books were expected to be of the same quality, and I can vividly recall the distress of a master who found Mr. Eliot's Poems, *South Wind*, and *Antic Hay* in my study. He had not heard of Mr. Eliot, but surely the other two were 'rather unhealthy writers'.

school time-table, which always gives the impression
of being designed to allot some compulsory activity
to every moment of the day, on the assumption (in
most cases a valid one) that when a boy finds that he
has no opportunity for acting at any moment as his
own inclination might suggest, he will abandon the
attempt to think for himself shortly after he has
shelved the attempt to act. It is interesting, too, to
note the official distrust of solitude, and the precautions that are taken to ensure that a boy has no
opportunity for doing anything in privacy. To my
mind this is the most pernicious feature in Public
School life. Meals are taken in a crowd, work is
done in a crowd, the team-spirit is encouraged in a
crowd on the playing-fields (it is curious, by the way,
that such stress should be laid in one place on the
team-spirit, and when two boys adopt the principle
for use in the class-room the result should be stig-
matized as 'Cheating'), bathing is permitted only in
a crowd, hours of presumptive leisure cannot be spent
alone (there were rarely less than three and sometimes
as many as six boys to a study about the size of a
Carthusian cell; this method of herding is generally
justified on the ground of limited space, to which it
may be replied that houses should be larger, or the
number of their inmates smaller), on wet days a House
Run brought sixty boys, of different ages, powers of
endurance and speeds in a uniform sweating mass up
the hillside and back; in the O.T.C.[1] the crowd-cult

[1] Theoretically, of course, a voluntary organization; in practice offering
slightly less opportunity for free choice than an election under Nazi rule.
During the whole time that I was at school I never heard of anyone being

reaches its apotheosis, when the whole school is united in one place in a single movement under military discipline. In my house the one opportunity for privacy that I think is general elsewhere was denied, as the lavatories had not been equipped with doors. Six latrines stood in a row in an ill-favoured pent-house in the yard, exposed to the view from in front and with only a thin partition between them. To the average new-boy, the victim of taboo from waist to knees as a result of the criminal neglect of biological rationalization that obtains in the English family and the English Preparatory School, it was not a reassuring arrangement. It might, however, have been an effective and valuable method of divesting the processes of elimination of the usual morbid embarrassment, if adequate instruction had been given to remove the common confusion that unites sexual matters with the eliminatory processes. The instruction was not given, and both subjects remained in the same category of taboo; officially unmentionable, and therefore the general topics of unsupervised conversation. In point of fact, I believe that the disposal of the lavatories was

asked whether he had any objection to joining. A possible explanation of this is that any boy with a knowledge of the subject might have objected on the grounds that he did not want his physique ruined for life. It has been abundantly proved (by, for instance, Col. H. E. Deans in *The Irritable Heart in Soldiers* and by scientific investigation in Australia and several countries in Europe) that the stiff and jerky movements and the rigid positions enforced in military drill are injurious, particularly to the still growing body.

I am glad to say that the O.T.C. was pretty generally disliked at Malvern. It therefore had the merit of converting at any rate a minority to a dislike of militarism. The sadist (whose happy hunting-ground the O.T.C. was) would however be entrenched in militaristic convictions. It is a point of psychological interest that some of the masters who showed eagerness to act as officers in the O.T.C. were those who in the rest of school life were the most inconspicuous and least assertive.

not an attempt at rationalization, but a precaution against their being used as a refuge for homosexuals. To my knowledge it succeeded as ill in this as it was demonstrably effective in stimulating exhibitionism.

The objection to homosexuality is fundamentally not a question of ethics but a question of orthodoxy, except in so far as orthodoxy is considered as identical with morality. The Public Schools confess (and some of them confess it with pride) that they do not cater for 'abnormal' boys. When they speak of 'character' (which they do, in the context of 'development', with monotonous frequency) they mean, not a well-developed personal identity in which the idiosyncrasies of the individual have been fused with a sense of obligation to the community, but a composite of certain standardized qualities, more frequently invoked than analysed, in whose perpetuation the system has a vested interest. The boy who exhibits noticeable affection for another boy offends by his unorthodoxy more than by his specific conduct, in that he demonstrates that he has not been moulded into the standard condition of insentient asexuality at which the system aims. The system is thus threatened with a failure to standardize: if it thinks that the affection is merely romantic, it does its best to suppress it; if it suspects that it is more, it retaliates by thrashing or expelling the rebel (sometimes by doing both). The fact that homosexuality is a natural and transitory condition of adolescence, and that the very conditions of school life designed to suppress it are the ones most likely to produce homosexual fixation, is naturally not recognized nor taken into consideration. What is least to the credit of the Public Schools is that it is generally attachments that have grown on a valuable and fertilizing basis of common interests and temperamental compatibility that are noticed and penalized, while the grosser examples of physical lust, being of their essence fugitive and secret, pass undetected.

An affection between a master and a boy is, in the conditions of school life, less likely to exist and less suspect if it does (the master, in most cases, being a properly conditioned Public School man himself). But the possibility is discouraged as much as possible, and such intimacy as does occur, being inhibited, is as a result generally furtive and sentimentalized. To my mind this is one of the main defects of Public School life. There can only be a completely satisfactory result from teaching when affection is permitted to exist between master and pupil. The mind is not an isolated machine that can function independently of the rest of the human system, and the capacity of a boy to profit from education is dependent upon his attitude to his teacher. The boy who is indifferent to his master's general personality can react to his teaching only in a restricted way. When his attitude is hostile, his response, if existing at all, will be merely negative. The relationship of masters and boys to-day is no doubt an improvement on the past. The master who, as a mildly superior being, takes pains to be on good terms with his pupils and to treat their deficiencies with good humour is not so rare a phenomenon as he used to be. He is not ideal, but there is no link of comparison between him and that pernicious creature (not yet obsolete) who acquires a second gown of dignity when he steps on to the dais: if he influences his pupils at all, it is merely as a textbook which happens to have the power of speech. I think it is fair to say that he is growing rarer. But the master who can meet his pupils without any patronage at all, either shown or felt, is, in the circumstances of Public School life, almost an impossibility. There were two at Malvern within my experience who perhaps came as near to the ideal as those circumstances would allow. Anything that I learned in the sixth form that I have found of value was learned from them, and between them and some of their pupils (and between one other master and the members of the house in which he was house-tutor) existed the only valuable affection that I saw while I was at school. On the other hand intimacy of precisely the wrong kind, relaxed officialdom, was comparatively common. I can remember the kind of fluctuating coquetry (the dignity of a glorified prefect always present in the background) that existed between one or two less responsible newcomers to the staff and some of the more flirtatious long-lease tenants of the Middle School. But it was nothing more than the testament of official restriction.

And the future? Perhaps a remedy for the present state of affairs would lie in increasing the difficulty of the entrance examination, and thus removing the necessity of moulding inborn stupidity into a standardized form which (in its present state) will be of steadily decreasing value to society. Not every boy can profit from education at the level which the Public Schools should be able to attain, and whatever the substitute should be for those who cannot, it is certainly not the training in reactionary conventionalism which the Public Schools now instil. The primary function of a school should be to create a satisfactory society for children to live in, the second, to provide a suitable introduction to adult life in the world. The Public Schools do neither. To some extent their limitations have been imposed by the incompatibility of the different elements they have tried to fuse. Not all the prizes of life, however, still go automatically to their products. Still less will go in the future, unless they are brought up to date. The strongholds of privilege are being opened to the products of other systems. If the Public Schools are to survive at all as institutions, it will be with different objects in view, with different methods, and with different material. As soon as the necessity for dragooning those who are naturally unfitted for the education they must provide has been removed, some of the absurdities of present methods of teaching, the barbarities of existing discipline, and the anachronisms of the present curriculum could be discarded. The curriculum should be related to the developments of civilization and changes in society. I am not suggesting that the Public Schools should become Technical Colleges (though certainly it should be possible for anyone already decided on a technical career to study subjects that may be of value to him in it), merely that their attitude should be contemporary, and that they should take steps to inculcate a civic sense other than that which is implicit in the present indoctrination of reactionary convention and conservative prejudice. It is not the function of an educational institution to impose any single creed of political belief, and I suspect that some of the otherwise admirable 'Progressive' Schools err in this respect. The civic sense implies the ability to think for oneself and to work by oneself, and as much as possible of freedom of thought and action, and leisure for private work, are essential. The prefect-system, as it is at present constituted, and a relationship between masters and boys which, as I have tried to suggest, combines some of the least desirable features of monasticism, feudalism and militarism, should be terminated. Above all, corporal punishment should be abolished. Possibly, however, this custom will fall automatically into disuse. The tradition of corporal punishment grew up side by side with the tradition of unmarried masters. It is a matter of medical observation that to a repressed and morbid man (as many masters in that monastic period were) whipping a boy frequently brings a feeling of acute sexual release. Instances of corporal punishment obviously inflicted for other than disciplinary reasons are too numerous in the history of English education to need insisting upon. It is interesting to note that with the increasing number of married masters, there has been a decline in the amount of corporal punishment inflicted.

Meanwhile we still have the Public School Boy, the product of the present system (the minority which has never absorbed the principles of the system remains outside consideration): at his best a practical man, a little limited in his views but tolerant towards those of different opinion, well mannered and polite, neat in his appearance and punctual in his ways, a shade superficial perhaps but perfectly adapted to climb gradually to the top of any of the professions for which he has been produced, a smoothly turning cog in the machine; at his worst a complacent philistine, unable to think for himself and leaning on a code for moral conviction, lacking in imagination and in vision, eager for popularity, emotionally dwarfed and blandly adolescent in sexual matters, insensitive to beauty and confused towards truth, a creature lost to progress in his obsequiousness towards convention, his inability for innovation, his class-consciousness and smug confidence in his own superiority, his faith in his own powers at a crisis ('It was the Public Schools which pulled the country through in the General Strike'), his narrowness and prejudice, above all his absurd Loyalty: 'I have to thank the Old School for making me what I am.'

PIONEERS

[Bedales]

BY E. L. GRANT WATSON

WHAT chance led my mother to send me to Bedales at the age of ten, I do not know, but I well remember the occasion of my first visit. After seeing over the school, we had supper with Mr. Powell, the second master, who lived in the little lodge at the gates of the school estate. He was a strange sort of man, I thought, to be a schoolmaster, and different from any man I had met before. I instinctively feared his alert, vigorous manner; he had strikingly blue eyes which looked at me very hard and made me feel that they were stern rather than kind. I received the impression that he thought me a puny little kid who would want a lot of bucking-up. He wore clothes unlike other men's, a pale blue tweed suit with leather at the cuffs, grey stockings and a red tie, and on his feet were very large home-made leather sandals. Everything in his house was very clean; the walls were whitewash with few pictures; there was plain oak furniture and bare boards. After the evening meal, Mr. Powell went into the kitchen to help his wife wash-up.

At my first meeting with the head master, the thought came with a flash that he was like Jesus

Christ. This may have been the cut of his beard, but there seemed to be more to account for it than that, for I got the impression that he was very just and pure and unselfish, yet at the same time, I felt rather than reasoned, that he was to be feared and respected rather than loved. I was shocked at my sacrilegious comparison, for Jesus was for me a figure of the imagination and not to be brought into the ordinary world of experience. If Mr. Powell had seemed strange and forbidding, Mr. Badley filled me with an even greater awe, and my first impressions were deepened at the school service on Sunday evening when he gave the address. His deliberate speech, the slow weighing of his words, and the rhythmical repetitions held me in a kind of painful suspense.

In 1893 Bedales was started as a pioneer school for the children of those parents, who, in the words of John Locke, 'were so irregularly bold that they dare venture to consult their own reason in the education of their children, rather than rely on custom.' It was the aim of this new school to give an all-round education in place of the early specialization, which at that date still prevailed in public schools. Aptitude was put before mere knowledge, and to develop harmoniously the body and mind was considered more important than to obtain honours in examinations. Examinations were not, at that date, considered desirable; there was no system of marks or test-papers; versatility was more important than specialization; the young Bedalians were taught to turn their hands to all things, to make beds, clean windows and boots, cultivate gardens, make chairs and tables, milk cows and make butter. There was an emphasis on the dignity of all labour; no task was degrading. To give emphasis to this point, the elder boys cleaned out the earth-privies, under the direction of the head master, who did not on this, or on any other occasion, in the least unbend from his attitude of stern and dignified reserve. They wheeled the barrows into which Mr. Badley shovelled the excrement, and very full he would load them for small boys to wheel, for there was no pampering, no thought of weak hearts or of young muscles strained to lift barrows, swimming to the brim.

If a general education and a belief in the dignity of labour was the first thing insisted on, hardihood was certainly the second. The windows were always open, cold baths were the rule, even though we had to break the ice on the goose-cans. There was a run before breakfast, taken with a switch by one of the bigger boys. As soon as our names had been called over, away we would scamper. It was a race, and the last one or two got the switch. The afternoon runs were a more formidable ordeal, these also were taken with a switch, and how we hated them! We were to learn courage and endurance, and there was to be no complaining. The school life was to be an organic spontaneous thing, growing out of itself, and not too definitely controlled or moulded by the staff. Discipline was to be a natural growth, produced amongst the boys for their own instruction, and not imposed from above. In the enthusiasm of that early time, we younger boys had

too much of this experimental discipline enforced by
our elders.

There were only twenty-nine boys at Bedales when
I first went there, and the school was at the original
buildings near Hayward's Heath; there were no girls.
A large country house, standing in the midst of its
own estate, had been adapted for this experiment in
education. In the first years of its being, it was regarded with considerable suspicion and disapproval
by the surrounding neighbourhood. Mr. Badley was
looked upon as a Socialist and an Atheist, and both
the general roughness and untidiness in matters of
dress, and the flavour of moral uplift were anti-
pathetic to the average mind. The wildest stories
spread and were believed; and on one occasion the
local policeman called to see the murdered corpse of
a boy, which was reported to have been buried
secretly. Mr. Badley had the amused satisfaction of
producing the small boy in question very much alive
and unconcerned. Yet I think there was some excuse
for the hostility of the neighbourhood: we were in
those early days desperately untidy as regards clothes,
often running barefoot for the greater part of the
summer term, and the bullying, of which there was
far too much, must have been obvious to outsiders.

Mr. Badley was as much of an enigma to the neighbourhood as he was to most of us boys. During all my
time at Bedales, he continued to fill me with a mixture
of awe and reverence. Never would I have thought of
fooling during his classes, that would have seemed as
dangerous as pulling the whiskers of a lion, and as

irreverent as singing comic songs in church. When he came, stalking with his quick, silent tread, into the class-room there was immediate silence; if there happened to be a piece of paper lying on the floor, he would point to it without deigning to say a word, and the boy who was nearest would hurriedly pick it up and put it in its right place; if a window were shut, he would merely point to it, and it would be opened. When at length, through silence and gesture, the correct order had been established, the class would begin. To most of the subjects which he taught, he gave an interest, which, for me, was a kind of suspended excitement; his presence always made me nervous, but often pleasurably so, and subjects usually considered dull, such as grammar, he could make alive. At first he even made Latin attractive, though in its later stages, when more was expected than was usually forthcoming, I used to dread these classes so much that the days on which they occurred were overshadowed and blackened. He also taught literature and history. These classes were pure happiness, and I would watch the clock, envious lest the minutes should go too fast.

Of Mr. Powell I was more frightened than of Mr. Badley, for in those days he was feared for his sudden bursts of impatience. He taught German and singing, at both of which I was very bad. At singing I was nervous and incompetent, and would suffer agonies in being had out before the whole school and made to sing scales. I never sang them correctly, but I had to try. Mr. Powell conducted the singing with a little oak baton, and this he would rattle between the teeth of the boys who had not their mouths sufficiently wide open. I was terrified of both him and his baton, and never learnt to sing any better.

Mr. Rice, who taught science, was a relaxation. He was easy-going and a bad disciplinarian. We all liked him, and showed our appreciation by making his classes as difficult as possible. His red, jovial face seldom showed anything but a smile, and his slow apprehension was usually too late to prevent the tricks we played him. Mr. Grubb, the only other master at that time, was a tall young quaker: he had a large, knobbly head, wore spectacles and blushed easily; he taught mathematics, and went through many phases, at times being so persecuted that his life must have been almost unendurable. At other times he was much in favour. I think, at heart, most of us liked him, and knew that he was a staunch Bedalian, and very loyal to the school and its ideals.

That I was unhappy at Bedales for my first year was inevitable. I had been brought up too gently for so sudden a transition into roughness. Life was pitched in a high and valorous key; we were expected to play hard and live hard and not to complain, but to fight our own battles. There was not supposed to be any bullying; we were trusted to behave according to the evening prayer in which we prayed not to make another's life harder by unkindness or oppression. Nevertheless my first year contained much acute misery, and even the holidays were clouded by the thought that each day threw me nearer to the dreaded return. When the time came for going back, I was ill with nervousness, and my mother had all she could do to hearten me. Things were worse than she imagined, for in that first year I experienced fear, hatred and despair, and learnt to harbour a fierce longing for revenge. I lived in a state of continual fear, and became a cowed and miserable little creature, reduced to lying and skunking, quite abject, without pride, and with very little courage.

One of the things I most feared was passing through the changing-room when the big boys were changing into their games-clothes, or back into their house-things. We all had to change in this room, and it was then that those who were so disposed would smack their wet hands on the backs of smaller boys, making what they called 'trade-marks'. One trade-mark might well be borne, though it could hurt a good deal, but fifteen or twenty in succession, would bring tears to the eyes of most small boys.

In this changing-room there were also from time to time things called 'pies' which would fill me with an ecstasy of fear. Some middle-sized, unpopular boy would be thrown into one of the baths. Then all the small boys who could be caught were seized and thrown in on top of him, and the big boys, who were the makers of the pie, would jump on top, shout and sing songs and hit at any portion of the struggling mass with the heels of their slippers, and, so as to brighten things up from below, would turn on the hot water. Of course the wretched boy underneath fought as for his life, and the little boys, between the slippers from above and the fighting from below, had a poor time of it, and were soon all howling lustily. To be made into a pie was one of the worst things that happened.

This kind of thoughtless, brutal roughness was very contagious, and boys who were not naturally bullies were infected by it, and one of my best friends, used, as he went along the corridor where the lockers were, to swing his bunch of keys on a string, and bring them down on the head of any smaller boy who was in the least in his way. He was probably unaware how much keys, thus wielded, could hurt, and unaware of how his victim would creep away into the passage where the great-coats were kept, and there weep in secrecy.

If we were free to be bullied at Bedales, we were also able to taste freedom as boys in few other schools were able to taste it. We were allowed to go our own ways, and to dispose of our free-time very much as we wished. In the Summer terms there were long and glorious Sundays.

From eleven-thirty in the morning till seven-thirty in the evening we were free, provided that we got the head master to sign our leave-slips — and this was seldom refused. We could go where, and do what we liked. We could take lunch with us and be lost in the woods, or could go on bicycles to Chailey common, or to the river to try and catch water-rats, or to track the spoor of an otter, or to a favourite piece of marsh land where slow-worms were to be found. These delightful creatures were easily tamed. We carried them in our pockets, and took them to bed with us, or persuaded them to coil round our wrists like bracelets, their heads showing close to our coat-cuffs, and their little black tongues flickering in and out as though feeling the air.

As time passed many of the things that at first had

seemed hardships I began to enjoy. I enjoyed the running, and being a good runner seldom felt the switch. I loved the outdoor life and became a keen naturalist in a small way, and most of my energies were directed towards the woods or the downs. In the summer I was up as soon as it was light, and away to the woods at Scaynes Hill to visit my friend the game-keeper. No one seemed to mind what I did in these early hours, but I was dreadfully sleepy for class-work after breakfast. During Mr. Powell's German class, which was the second period, I was often so sleepy that I would doze off in spite of my fear of his wrath. In my classes I was very backward, and I believe our class-standard at that time was poor. I wrote and spelt abominably, and was considered a hopeless dunce. I was not, however, altogether a failure, and soon began to develop a keen school patriotism, and in so doing became deeply influenced by the strong school tone.

This school tone was, I think, the most remarkable thing about the early Bedales, and looking back at that time, it seems extraordinary how much a large number of the boys, and all the staff, were at one with the head master in his ideal of creating a wider, freer life. In so far as we were conscious of this, we were doubtless prigs, but I don't think that mattered very much; what was good about it, was that we felt ourselves to be part of the natural and developing growth of the school. We were part of a living organism, which had not yet turned into an institution. Bedales was making its own history, and if we lived through its

Dark Ages, we also knew its Renaissance, and it was the boys, just as much as the masters, if not more than the masters, who determined its phases. In our primitive society, we discovered the laws of our own evolution, and this constituted no unimportant portion of our education. That part of this process was difficult and mistaken, cannot be denied, but there were compensations to outweigh the disadvantages. What was, I believe, the worst thing about the strong school-tone was the very powerful prejudice against any sexual curiosity or adolescent sensuality. We were informed of the biological facts of sex, or some of them, but these were so spoken of, that they remained mental abstractions rather than emotional centres of interest. A strong tone of sexual purity was established, and in all the nine years of my time at Bedales, I came in contact with very little smut. This tone was so powerful that our sexual tendencies, which would normally develop in conscious curiosity and experiment, were not only effectively suppressed, but very largely repressed, with a consequent keying-up of the emotional life. I remember a well-meaning master from a public school commenting on what was in his eyes this extraordinarily satisfactory state of affairs. He remarked how far superior were the pure minds of the Bedalians to the corresponding little sinks of iniquity displayed by the average public-school boy. Little did he know of Freud!

As I grew older and stronger and worked my way up the school, I changed from the abject little creature of my first year into a normal school-boy. I was no longer bullied, but was able to pass on some of the bullying I had received, though I was never an exception in this respect, and have not many black deeds to reproach myself with. My energies were soon to be occupied in meeting the problems presented by the introduction of girls.

Before starting Bedales as a co-educational school, Mr. Badley discussed the change with some of the older boys, and enlisted their support. At that time I was in the lower middle school, and was of course not consulted. I very much resented the change, as did the other boys of my age. We thought it *infra dig.* to be at a school with girls, and were not surprised that quite a number of boys were taken away by their parents at the time the change was made. We dubbed the girls 'beastly shes' and set about to make their lives as intolerable as possible. At first there were only four girls, and I think they had a very rough time of it. We did not actually hit them or twist their arms, but we passed on what petty unkindnesses we thought safe, such as hacking of shins and pulling of hair. With shame I look back on my own attitude, and can only find excuse in the thought that it was part of a collective reaction against the new and the strange. This unpleasant phase did not last long; as we grew older our sentiments changed, and the 'beastly shes' became attractive in a strange and disturbing fashion. I remember very clearly the upswelling feeling when I first *saw* a girl, and recognized her as a human creature, different from a boy, and different from anything I had known before. I was coming down a narrow wooden stair and she was coming up. I had to stand aside to let her pass.

I had not noticed her much before, but when she was opposite me, we both paused. I looked at her, and saw that she was breathing hard from running and the big strides she was taking. Her cheeks were flushed; she looked at me and smiled, then gave a little laugh and ran on, and I was left standing on the stairs, wondering why she had suddenly seemed so different, and why my heart was beating faster than usual.

As the number of girls increased and as our initial hostility changed to interest, and from interest to that queer ambivalent feeling of attraction and dislike, love-affairs of various qualities and intensities made their appearance. It is not within the scope of this essay to discuss the merits or de-merits of co-education; that is far too large and controversial a subject, I only wish to recall memories. It was a time of experiment and change, and one of considerable difficulty for both masters and boys. The school was now growing rapidly larger and the staff was increased. The high moral tone, flavoured so strongly with idealism and sexual purity, was as firm set as ever. This argued considerable repression, and found its expression in a policy of retarding adolescence as far as possible. The young, unmarried members of the staff were as much troubled by the new experiment as were the boys, and most of us were very uncomfortably unconscious of what we were doing and what we were wanting. Love-affairs were discouraged and held up to ridicule as sentimental and silly. Yet in spite of this, and I think *because* of the high moral tone our emotional life was abnormally acute. We plunged pretty deeply into that alluring, exciting and most painful experience of first love. At least some of us did. Others, particularly the younger, unmarried masters, and some of the elder boys in their effort to cope with their own inner difficulties, took up an attitude of rigid Puritanism, which delighted, with a savage and vindictive pleasure, in scenting-out and persecuting the loving-couples that were less repressed than they. This time of experiment and discovery, for co-education in a boarding-school was quite new in England, was of necessity a difficult period, and one in which a good many mistakes were bound to be made. My own experience was, I believe, fairly typical, if any experiences can be said to be typical, where all are different and individual. I fell very much in love in a quite innocent and sentimental manner. For this I was persecuted, at the instigation of one of the younger masters. Of course I resented this, and put up a strong resistance, and produced clouds of emotion and indignation. The thing lasted some twelve months, and I was desperately miserable and angry. At the end I was completely worsted, and in my bitterness declared that I hated girls and all to do with them. Inevitably, almost automatically I joined the lover-persecuting fraternity.

Other boys had less difficulty and less painful experiences: their friendships with girls were not so deeply emotional, and they avoided the undesirable extremes that were the fate of the less fortunate. Changes took place fairly rapidly, and, with the passing generations of boys and masters, some of the worst difficulties were naturally sloughed off. The head master of course remained; and on looking back on my own rather troublous time, I see him as the one person who always took the lenient and the generous view. In his own person he did not seem to be identified with that rigorously puritanical tone that he appeared to have created. Often both masters and prefects were clamouring for the expulsion of some particularly difficult individual, but he would be for giving them another chance, and another, and yet another.

While these deep and far-reaching changes were taking place in the inner life of the school, it had so far expanded in numbers, that the old house at Haywards Heath was no longer large enough. The estate near Petersfield was bought and the new school was built. We moved in while the builders were still at work. Bedales was now no longer the small school of twenty-nine boys; it had four-times multiplied its numbers. There was less emphasis on the physical side of our life; we were no longer so cranky. More normal clothes were allowed and encouraged; compromises had been made with regard to examinations; our mental standard was improving, and instead of producing chiefly farmers and handicraftsmen, both boys and girls were sitting for scholarship examinations at the universities.

The old school, which I set out to write about, with its crankiness, its puritanism, and its idealistic enthusiasm, was already passing into the modern school, where co-education is no longer an experiment, but an established institution, and which is something very different indeed from the Bedales of the past.

A CHILD OF THE FIVE WOUNDS

['Lippington']

I

Soon after my book *Frost in May* had appeared, I received two letters from 'old children' of Lippington. One of the writers had left in 1883; the other in 1927; both were quite certain, from my description of the convent, that I must have been their contemporary. The fact that actually I left in 1914 is irrelevant; Lippington does not change. Reverend Mothers and Mistresses of Discipline may come and go, but their characters affect the school very little. The real ruler is an invisible one — the French saint who, in the early part of the nineteenth century, founded the Order of the Five Wounds and laid down, once and for all, its code of manners and morals.

II

I went to Lippington when I was eight. My first few weeks were as miserable as I expected them to be. I had to adapt myself to another new element besides that of a boarding-school — the difficult, rarefied element of the Catholic Faith. For I was a very raw

Catholic indeed. My father had been received into the Church only six months before, and, although I had learnt my catechism and made my first Confession, I had none of the Catholic manners and graces. I wore neither scapulars nor miraculous medals under my serge uniform; I could not boast of having been dedicated to Our Lady and dressed exclusively in blue and white for my first seven years; I had not even a patron Saint. Worse than that, I made mistakes which, for years after, caused me to turn cold with shame when I remembered them. I often made the Sign of the Cross with the wrong hand, forgot to genuflect to the Blessed Sacrament or bow my head at the Holy Name, and even finished the Lord's Prayer with the Protestant tag of 'for Thine is the kingdom, the power and the glory' instead of stopping short, as Catholics do, at 'deliver us from evil'. In fact, I was far more of an outsider than any of the foreign children. Spanish, Austrian, French and Polish girls, who could not speak a word of English, found their level at once. They might be inarticulate but the very way their trunks were packed, with a crucifix folded in tissue paper among the dozen regulation calico nightgowns, was proof of 'a good Catholic home' in the background.

III

Every day at Lippington was punctuated, at brief intervals, by bells and prayers. At half-past six the rising bell clanged through the corridors and was echoed by the tinkle of the 'sonnette' of the nun in charge. Her voice declaimed 'Precious Blood of Our Lord Jesus Christ' and from behind the white curtains of our cubicles we answered sleepily 'wash away our sins'.

I soon learnt to leap from my warm, narrow bed at the first clamour, for there was a tradition that such an act might help to release a soul from purgatory. In winter, if we put our wash-basins outside our cubicles, we received a meagre allowance of tepid water, but it was considered more in the spirit of the Order to wash in cold. Baths we had twice a week, but they were no ordinary baths. Before we stepped into them, although we bathed separately and behind locked doors, we had to envelop ourselves in huge calico cloaks which tied round our necks and hung in heavy folds to our feet. They protected us from the scandalizing sight of our naked bodies but they made washing difficult. Personally I never attempted to soap more than my face and hands and was contented to lie in the hot water, with my cloak swelling round me like an inflated balloon, until the bell rang for 'Out of your baths, children.'

Dressing was conducted behind closed curtains and on the same principles of modesty. We were taught to tie the sleeves of our nightgowns round our waists while we slipped on our vests so that, at no time, should we be entirely naked. A quarter of an hour after the rising bell, another tinkle warned us to emerge from our cubicles, in our flannel petticoats and dressing-gowns, to brush our hair in public. Looking glasses were, of course, forbidden, but we were allowed to make signs (never to speak) to a neighbour to find out whether our partings were straight. Hair was obliged to be worn plaited and strained back so stiffly from our foreheads that it drew our eyes up at the corners, Chinese fashion. And, once a week, a Lay-Sister went over our heads with a fine tooth-comb and drenched them with a vile-smelling yellow wash. Once a month, rather surprisingly, a young man came to shampoo us. We looked forward to this, not because of the young man (all of us, except a few foreigners, had a proper contempt for the other sex) but because we got off preparation for an hour and were allowed, during the drying process, to loosen the high starched collars that scored red rings round our necks.

Early Mass was at 7.15 and breakfast, a French breakfast of bread and butter and coffee, at 8. Except during Lent we were allowed to talk at meals (the only time we *could* talk, apart from recreation) but if we made too much noise, as we usually did, another bell commanded silence. The food was not calculated to make us greedy, but every morsel of hated fat and vinegar-soaked cabbage had to be eaten on pain of the whole table being kept in from games.

After breakfast, we made our beds and proceeded, always in orderly files, to the big study room for morning preparation. During this hour a curious custom was observed. If a child wished to go to the lavatory, she handed an orange card marked 'study' to the mistress in charge. The nun, having collected perhaps sixty of these cards, distributed them as she chose, and, until you had received back your card, you might not leave the room.

For the rest of the day, major and minor bells announced classes, meals, recreations and prayers. Each hour of study began with an invocation to the Holy Ghost and ended with a recommendation to Our Lady. Three times a day we recited the Angelus and, at half-past six, the whole school assembled for the rosary or for prayers to the patron saints of hygiene, St. Philomena and St. Roch. After supper came a brief indoor recreation, then night prayers in the chapel and bed. We undressed with another ritual of bells and our last spoken words, like our first, were 'Wash away my sins'.

At first I used to curl up in bed for warmth as I did at home but I was cured of this evil habit by an old French nun.

'Suppose, my child,' she said gently, 'that you died in the night. Would that be a becoming posture in which to meet Our dear Lord?'

And she taught me to lie on my back 'like a Christian' with my feet thrust well down into the cold sheets and my hands crossed on my chest. She taught me, too, to imitate St. Theresa by letting my last thoughts dwell on the Agony in the Garden, and to murmur the name of Jesus just before I fell asleep.

I V

It is a great mistake to suppose that children in a school like Lippington are unhappy, or even that their

spirits are crushed. Up to a point high spirits were
encouraged and, during my first term I was often
teased by the nuns for not showing sufficient 'natural,
healthy naughtiness'. One thing however was severely
stamped out of us — any tendency towards a
dangerous independence of mind. Through years of
training, the nuns had learnt to recognize the faintest
signs of such an attitude, and it was severely repressed.
They could detect it in the slightest thing — a straying
curl, an inclination to 'answer back' and, most of all,
in the faintest hint of speculation in matters of faith.
The world was waiting for us outside with its Satan-
set traps of heresy, free thought and easy morals, and
the whole object of our education was to arm us
against its snares. Mental pride and physical vanity
were considered the most dangerous of all our temptations and our mistresses were always on the watch for
their appearance. I do not agree that their sharp way
of dealing with them was due to any sadistic impulse.
Given the Catholic way of looking at things, there was
no more personal cruelty in it than in the drawing of a
poisoned tooth.

Nor, though we lived in perpetual consciousness of
religion, were we often worried by the thought of
hell-fire. During retreats there were certainly some
harrowing sermons on eternal punishment but, after
all, we knew very well how to avoid it. No one goes
to hell who does not die in mortal sin and we were all
firmly resolved never to commit such a thing. Indeed,
in those days, a mortal sin would have presented
itself not merely as an imprudence but as an actual

difficulty. In my nightly 'examination of conscience' I could always discover two of the main ingredients, in the day's faults, full knowledge and full consent but never the third and most important one, grave matter.

In the Junior School, especially, we were encouraged to look on the bright side of Catholic theology. Our Lady, the saints and the angels were real people to us — friends to whom we could look for sympathy and encouragement, whom we could even reverently tease. I soon learnt to pray to St. Anthony when I lost my pencil or my hair-ribbon, to seek the aid of Our Lady of Good Success in the weekly examinations, to promise St. Cecilia a novena if she got me into the choir. Every night I confided the day's troubles to my guardian angel and smoothed a place for him on my pillow so that he could watch over me in comfort. I began to recognize all round me the signs of heaven on earth. The cross on the donkey's back was a reminder of the Entry into Jerusalem; the cock at the farm crowed 'Christus natus est', the cows lowed 'Ubi . . . ubi?' and the sheep bleated 'Be-e-ethlehem.'

In those blue-pinafored days, before we were promoted to the black serge *tablier* of the Senior School, the rule was 'small penances . . . quick rewards'. Any genuine attempt at neatness or diligence brought its recompense — a sweet wrapped in pink paper, permission to read *Little Folks*, visit the bakery (where the beetles so often got baked into the bread), pick flowers for the altar or dress the statue of the Holy Child in His best tinsel robe and crown for a feast-day. We were not bullied, but coaxed, into virtue. At intervals, if there had been a notable falling off in manners, silence, or obedience, we would have a special 'practice' to strengthen us in it. We would be enrolled as Knights of Our Lady wearing silver shields inscribed with 'Noblesse Oblige'; as medieval champions tracking down the dreadful dragon of disobedience; as English martyrs practising the heroic virtue of silence on the rack.

v

Each term had its own special character. The autumn one began badly, after the long summer holidays, when we had got a little out of training and were inclined to be rebellious and homesick. But it warmed up as Christmas approached (we began to look forward to it about the first of October) and towards the end of it came one of the pleasantest feasts of the year, the Immaculate Conception. The 'old children' came back in full force for this and, with their worldly clothes and unrepressed chatter and shrill 'do you remembers', they were an exciting element. All of us, at least all who did not intend to become nuns, looked forward to the day when we could sweep about the corridors in long skirts and spotted veils and sable muffs, and we could not understand their passion for dressing up in old uniforms whenever they had the chance. The stone passages were decorated for the 'eighth' with garlands of evergreen and Chinese lanterns, and the smell of laurel and burning candles for once overcame the typical Lippington smell of beeswax, tea-leaves and incense. At the close of the day we filed two by two past the picture of Mater Admirabilis in the Lady Chapel and dropped white cotton lilies into a basket, saying 'Oh, Mary, I give you the lily of my heart, be thou its guardian for ever.' The lilies symbolized our Purity, but I think we were all a little hazy as to what Purity really meant. We knew that it was very important but that it was not *convenable* to talk about it.

The Spring Term was always a wretched one, for it brought Lent and, for us, Lent was a depressing reality. We did not fast, of course, but we ate a great deal of boiled cod which tasted no better for being eaten in silence. The nuns, we knew, not only fasted for the full six weeks, but endured all sorts of penances as well. What these were we could only guess; there were rumours of hair shirts and spiked belts. Once I saw a nun reach up to take a book from a high shelf; her sleeve fell back and I noticed small chains bound tightly round her arms. There was a gloomy, penitential air about all those weeks and many of us prayed quite frankly for an epidemic to break the monotony. Our prayers were usually answered.

But the summer months almost made up for Lent. The term was thickly strewn with major feasts and there were glorious holidays when we played hide-and-seek with the novices up and down the lime-shaded alleys, and when we were allowed to read thrilling secular books instead of the usual lives of the saints — such books as *Carrots*, *Jan of the Windmill* and rather surprisingly, Fr. Rolfe's *Stories Toto told me*. There would be chocolates and weak currant wine at dinner and the day would end with some dazzling entertainment; fireworks by the lake, charades, performing dogs hired from Whiteleys, or, best of all, a ghost story told, in pitch darkness, by one of the nuns. Ghost stories were a great feature of Lippington and there were at least five born story-tellers in the community. The fact that there was always a moral attached, such as that one must never miss Sunday Mass or become a Freemason, did not prevent them from being larded with good sound horrors. Huddling close together on the floor and even, under cover of the darkness, daring to disobey a strict rule by clutching a friend's hand, we listened breathlessly to tales of tortures, murders, skeleton hands and lost brides crumbling to dust in cellars. We enjoyed them immensely and thought them well worth an occasional nightmare.

VI

The Order, as I have said before, was founded by a saint. But she was a French saint and a woman of the world. The first object of the Five Wounds had been to provide a good education for the daughters of the French aristocracy. Certain formal graces still clung to our manners. Nuns in the higher positions had to be greeted, wherever we met them, with a deep curtsey. When we saw our parents in the parlour on Sundays and Thursdays we had to wear our lisle thread gloves. The parlour had once been a ballroom

in the big eighteenth-century house, and a certain
faded elegance still clung to its parquet floor and stiff
lace curtains. On entering it, we made no less than
three curtseys — one to our own relatives, one to
the other children's, and a third to the *surveillante* in
charge.

At the back of our Mother Foundress' mind had been
the idea that many of us would one day marry. She
had great faith in the influence of good wives and
mothers and a great sense of social dignity. Though
personal vanity was sternly discouraged, neatness of
hair and clothes and grace of movement were
respected. I wonder in how many secular schools in
1914 Deportment was still being taught as an art?
We went further than that; we even had several
backboards in the study-room, and anyone suspected
of a round back had to recline on their slippery
surface for half an hour a day.

Once a week we were visited by the Deportment
Mistress, an elderly Frenchwoman with a brassy wig
and the smallest black-satin-shod feet I have ever
seen. Clapping her fat little hands together and crying
'Graces, Graces, to your places' or 'Alack, alack, what
a deplorable back' she would shepherd us through the
motions of the *grande révérence*, the minuet, entering
and leaving a room, greeting a friend at a soirée,
performing an introduction and gracefully ignoring
an unwanted acquaintance.

We learnt a little dancing, mainly mazurkas and
quadrilles, but in response to the demands of some
of the more worldly parents, Reverend Mother reluc-

tantly allowed the elder ones to learn the Valse. It was a rigid affair, that Valse. We danced it, not in silk frocks, but in our clumsy serge uniforms and cotton gloves and thick black stockings, and, as in no circumstances were we allowed to encircle each other's waist, each girl held her partner stiffly at arm's length, as, a full yard apart, the couples gyrated slowly round the room.

The mazurkas were more fun. I can still see a fierce, blue-eyed girl, from Warsaw, who was always declaring that she would wade through seas of blood to restore the freedom of Poland, stamping her heels and shaking her long fair plait, in a perfect fury of abandon to Chopin's music.

VII

Lippington was, officially, an English school. But the old French tradition was stronger than any new-fangled, British notion about 'leaving girls on their honour'. True, the nuns talked about 'honour' but they were too wise to trust to so frail a reed. We were kept under the most rigid *surveillance* and, even when we believed ourselves alone, a nun would appear from nowhere, in her noiseless list slippers, to make sure that we were not getting into mischief. On the assumption that 'when two are together, the devil makes a third' we never walked in pairs but always in trios. Outgoing and incoming letters were opened and censored; desks, pockets and workboxes were liable to inspection at any moment. When I took my weekly piano lesson with my old music-master, it was always with an open door and in the presence of a *surveillante*.

We were not allowed to possess any book without permission. In my first term, my father gave me a Bible. But, although it was the orthodox Douay version, it was promptly banished to my trunk. The reason was simple. The nuns said, quite rightly, that the Bible contains many passages quite unsuitable for the eyes of any girl under eighteen and, to this day, I have never read the whole of the Old Testament. Even our school poetry books, chosen by the authorities themselves, had several pages cut out of them. I remember that Browning's 'Last Ride Together', Shelley's 'I arise from dreams of Thee', and the fourth Canto of Dante's Inferno were among the suppressions. The National Song Book was another trap; it was not actually mutilated, but there were several apparently innocent songs, of which we were never allowed to sing more than the first verse. One day we were given 'The Little Red Lark' to read at sight but the mistress stopped us after a few bars.

'I am sorry, children,' she said, 'I had only looked at the music of this song, not at the words. Will you please turn immediately to another page?'

And I remember a child in the Junior School (she came from a blameless Catholic home) who was given 'The Water Babies' for a birthday present. It was burnt, but no shame attached to the recipient. Her parents had obviously forgotten that it was on the Index.

VIII

Most people laugh at a Convent education. In my own experience it was at least as good as, if not better than, the one which I received later at 'the best type of English High School.' At Lippington it was hoped that none of us would ever fall into such dire necessity as to be forced to earn our own living, so we competed for no public examinations. We were educated, purely and simply, for a civilized and leisured life. The curriculum may have been narrow, the outlook biased, but the teaching was admirable and there was no lesson at Lippington that I did not thoroughly enjoy. The excellent digests of other people's books which were later crammed into me at St. Paul's and which enabled me to pass Cambridge Higher Local have left no impression whatever on my mind, but I have never forgotten anything I learnt at Lippington. Languages, music, and the history of painting were taught with far more intelligence and efficiency at the Five Wounds than at any ordinary secular school and we also learnt such old-fashioned, but useful accomplishments as reading aloud and writing tolerable letters. Literature, it is true, was taught with many reservations, but well enough to give us a genuine love of it and the elements of a respectable taste. In the matter of writing I owe a great deal to that education and I may as well admit it. I have not used my pen for purposes of which the Lippington authorities would approve but, were it not for them, I should probably never have used it at all.

IX

The Lippington system, in all but a few cases, produced its intended effect. We were expected to leave at eighteen or nineteen, with strong convictions and still stronger habits of mind, to marry young and to hand on the Catholic tradition to a large family. I often wondered what would have happened to me if I had run the full course of the Five Wounds training. But, on my fourteenth birthday, a terrible disaster befell me. For some months before that I had been a puzzle to the nuns and to myself. Outwardly I had behaved quite well, even to the point of being awarded the coveted green ribbon for good conduct. But, deep inside me, a tough little core of rebelliousness was growing. I was hardly aware of it myself, but the nuns, with their infallible eyes, knew all about it and watched me with suspicion. The saints began to have less and less attraction for me, and the poets more and more. I soaked myself in Francis Thompson, wrote passionate essays, and, in the Christmas holidays read *Dorian Gray*, which lit in me an uncontrollable desire to write a novel. A convenient epidemic in the spring term gave me my chance. Isolated in the 'Retreat House' I wrote three burning chapters. It was meant to have an extremely moral ending in which the heroine became a Carmelite and the hero a Jesuit, but I thought it would be more exciting if I made them all very bad at first. Accordingly, the hero (remembering *Dorian Gray*) wrapped himself in a yellow dressing-gown 'of some subtle

Levantine silk, wrought with strange embroideries' and the heroine, who had lips 'like a scarlet geranium,' kissed a total stranger on a balcony 'to the wild, throbbing strains of a Hungarian band'.

Vanity was my downfall. I could not resist showing the three chapters to my best friend. Next day there was one of those sudden, secret inspections of desks and the manuscript disappeared. But nothing was said. For a week of torturing suspense I waited. It was Holy Week and never had the ceremonies seemed so interminable. The castastrophe did not come until Easter Sunday which coincided that year with my birthday. I was actually lighting the candles on my cake when I was summoned to the parlour, not the ordinary friendly parlour, but the gloomy Community one, with its dark serge hangings and forbidding portraits. The interview with my father was one which, after twenty years, I don't care to remember. I was given no chance to explain the magnificent conversions I had arranged for the later chapters; I was accused of perversity, corruption and indecency. And I was told that, though I was not officially expelled, I must leave the school at once.

After my parents had left and I still sat on, battered and weeping, the nun who had been responsible for my disgrace came and talked to me. She explained, quite kindly, that I needed a humiliation of this kind. The fact that I had written something silly and vulgar was almost irrelevant; the real fault lay in my essential vanity and stubbornness. As she put it 'Our own wills can do nothing but harm unless they are humbly united to the will of God. And your will, my dear child, little by little, has been growing away from Him. Spiritual pride is the greatest of all sins and it must be rooted out, however much it hurts us. Your will had to be broken and re-set in God's own way.'

x

I went on, not to another house of the Five Wounds, as the nuns had suggested, but to St. Paul's Girls' School. After Lippington it was difficult to take any school very seriously. The gentle social pressure of 'good form' and 'loyalty' meant absolutely nothing to me; in a mild way I behaved outrageously. The relief of getting away from uniform was such that I never wore a 'gym tunic' unless compelled to and burst out into the brightest colours and the most unsuitable clothes. Although I was only fourteen, I felt far older than any of the prefects. I refused to play games, did very little work, patronized everybody and generally made a nuisance of myself. In spite of this, everyone treated me with the kindness English people show to lunatics, and I had rather a good time.

But, if I had no loyalty to my new school, my loyalty to the Church was more fervent than ever. I became more Catholic than the Pope; carved my desk with pious mottoes and festooned myself with scapulars. My history essays had a Catholic bias which would have shocked even Mr. Belloc; I invariably wrote Protestant with a small 'p' and always spoke of 'Good Queen Mary' and 'Bloody Bess'. But, at heart,

I felt *déclassée* and an exile. I had forfeited the rights of a Child of the Five Wounds. I went back at intervals to see the nuns, and watched other children, in dark blue uniforms, walking about under the plane-trees and munching their *goûter* of bread and jam as they listened to the old stories about their Mother Foundress. But, though they received me very kindly, the situation was false and strained. It was a relief when the heavy door shut behind me and I was back again in the suburban lane, in the world to which I, an outsider from first to last, really belonged.

THE LAST WORD

[Berkhamsted]

THE final sentence of Mr. Harold Nicolson's essay will probably be echoed by many of our unfavourable critics. 'All this was true once; but to-day it is out of date: "things" have changed.' When people speak of 'things' changing, they refer, of course, not to what is praised but to what is condemned. What Mr. Auden finds to admire in Holt, Mr. Powell in Eton, Mr. Hartley in Harrow, Mr. Spender in University College School is taken as permanent; the public schools, these critics believe, are slowly but surely progressing towards perfection, particularly now that education is in the hands of younger men.

But the young head master is not necessarily more open to modern ideas than the middle-aged (the type of young man likely to appeal to a middle-aged board of governors is not perhaps the most progressive). He has gone straight from his school to a university, where he is probably a loyal member of his old Boys' Society, and straight back to a school again. Once there he spends all his time with his fellow masters, even his holidays (witness a recent disaster in Switzerland). I don't know at what point he comes in contact with modern ideas.

I am thinking of my own school. I do not believe that it is family pride which makes me admire the head master's achievement (he is my father). He was an admirably progressive head master, never more so than in his later years at the school. A great many of the reforms which the progressive schools still regard as daring innovations could be found working smoothly at Berkhamsted. The masters were allowed an unusually free hand if they wished to experiment. An enthusiast was even allowed to start a system of self-government. It failed (you cannot be a socialist in a capitalist state), but he was given time and sympathy for his experiment. I remember with gratitude the admirable chamber concerts . . . Discipline was as humane as you could find anywhere outside a progressive school. Only house-masters were allowed to cane, neither prefects nor form-masters. It was not a really satisfactory school for sadists; only two sadistic masters come back to mind, and one of them was so openly sadistic, so cheerful a débauchee, that one could not grudge him his pleasure. Boys, like whores, prefer a man who enjoys shamelessly what he is about.

But my father retired, a young man was appointed, and it was the young man who preferred to follow the older tradition. More time was given to games and less to work, physical training ceased to be a serious part of the curriculum, prefects were given the right to cane. What this may mean in the way of sexual indulgence even Mr. Hartley's blithe attitude to 'whoppings' does not disguise.

228

That is an example of the young head master. Here is another example, an article in the *Spectator* addressed to parents by Mr. P. H. B. Lyon, head master of Rugby. 'What you ought to tell Kenneth before he goes back to his old school.' In its sentimentality, its complacency, its uneasy attitude to sex, it might have been written by Dean Farrar. It is as much a period piece as *Eric*:

'I am coming, you may have suspected, to the one thing about which you possibly want advice more than any other, the question of sex. Now here the first thing necessary is an unostentatious appeal to a decent boy's fastidiousness; this is a fine first defence against all evil. Kenneth will, I believe, instinctively shy at the first suggestion of "smut"; what you can do is to reassure him that such aversion is not cowardice, that nothing noble or manly lies along that road. But this is not enough; innocence must be reinforced by knowledge of the right kind, before knowledge of the wrong kind overpowers it. Before long Kenneth should be told quietly, naturally, and fully, the physical facts of marriage and birth, with some word of the spiritual experience which accompanies and transforms them; something, too, of his own growing powers and temptations. If this is done aright he will be equipped with reverence, chivalry, self-respect, three fine weapons. Who is to do this? Not you, my dear G., nor your good wife, unless one or both of you have from the first talked naturally with him about everything. If the subject raises a barrier of reserve between you, then you may do more harm than good in your effort to break it down. For myself, I think a boy's house-master should add this to his many duties; let us hope "Fishface" thinks the same. He would do it well, being (as I have said) a kind and sensible man, who has probably expounded these mysteries to innumerable small boys in his time.'

Really, it would be possible to read Mr. Lyon without ever guessing that sexual intercourse was pleasant or amusing. You recognize the old idea; sex is dirty, but if it's called marriage, it's much too sacred to be talked about in public.

After reading the essays in this book, I very much doubt Mr. Lyon's complacent statement in the same article that Kenneth 'will have his dragons to fight, but they won't be of his school's making.' To me there emerges from these essays more than anything else the great importance of individuals to the schoolboy's happiness, while the system, by which I mean the rules, routine and tradition of the school, seems generally designed only for the convenience of the authorities and often works for the boy's unhappiness. How often the happiest memories in these essays are of friendships with individual masters, seldom with boys, for there too often the system interferes with its cult of suspicion and its abnormal fear of sexuality.[1]

[1] This coincides with my own experience. I remember with the deepest gratitude my English lessons with X., a classical master, who for one year took a small group of boys in extra English lessons for the Higher Certificate examination. We wrote him bad short stories and still worse verses, he read us parts of *Death's Jest Book* in his nasal deeply expressive drawl, and we felt ourselves in contact for almost the first time with a really civilized

I except the co-educational schools, and to some extent Eton and Harrow which seem to combine extraordinary barbarity in their discipline with a really civilized attitude of trust. Few schools can afford to give separate rooms to every boy: fewer schools still would give them even if they had the money.

I cannot believe that my own school, so progressive in many ways, was peculiar in its mistrust, the attitude that privacy could only be misused, the attitude of the divorce courts. Lavatories in my house had no locks, so that even that opportunity for a little quiet reading or writing was denied, and as there were no individual studies, the boy, whatever his age, whatever his intellectual inclinations, passed the greater part of each year (thirty-eight out of fifty-two weeks) in an atmosphere of clamour (how can thirty boys in a small common-room not make a noise?) and smells (the excessive sexual purity of my house vented itself in the crudest of scatological jokes). How under those conditions can any boy be expected not to work off his irritation and boredom in bullying? Not even at night has he the sense of being alone. In a large dormitory hardly a quarter of an hour passes without

literate mind. The relief to the nerves was intense, to realize one was not alone in believing that to try to write English well was more important than to try to play cricket well.

We were unlikely to get that idea from the other English masters: Y., who taught by rote (I learned from him that one must not end a sentence with a preposition; that sentences should all be short, or perhaps that sentences should all be long); or Z., a popular Welshman, who set us to paraphrase the loveliest passages in *King Lear* and who once read us Shelley's 'Question' aloud, so that we might write down immediately afterwards as many of the flowers mentioned in the poem as we could remember. The boy who remembered most was top in English that day.

someone snoring or talking in his sleep. This intense inescapable communal life cannot be good for anyone. The least sensitive, the most sociable boy surely needs the opportunity to be alone.

Let me be just. The school was poor; the houses were correspondingly poorer. The house-masters could not have given the boys more room if they had wanted to. What was wrong was a tradition of supervision which made them disinclined to ease those conditions in other ways. Even locks on the lavatory doors would have been something, though I suppose after reading Mr. Verschoyle's account of Malvern we should have been grateful for doors. I wonder what they imagined might go on behind locked doors? One is alternately amazed at the unworldly innocence of the pedagogic mind and at its tortuous obscenity.

Solitary walks too were forbidden. Each Sunday a notice was pinned on the gymnasium door giving the names of the boys walking together. On the first evening of term one went round filling up a kind of dance programme of walks for the term. The mental agony of a boy with a limited number of friends who failed to book all his walks was, of course, extreme. He would not be allowed to walk by himself and would have to impose himself or be imposed on others. What the house-master gained by this it is difficult to understand, except a comforting illusion that he knew whom everyone was with. In practice it was perfectly easy to arrange with another boy to start out together and then separate. A foolish rule like so many others not peculiar, I am sure, to my own school: the not very hygienic rule, for example, that caps must always be worn outside the school premises. My father's predecessor, who became Dean of Lincoln and in the words of obituary writers 'a great Christian', flogged a boy for appearing at school without his cap. As a training for life indeed the school was not more efficient than other public schools. It taught a moral standard quite out of keeping with adult manners. Mr. Auden's essay reminded me that we too had the silly, but for our supervisors convenient, tradition of owning up. A hypocritical tradition, for who in later life 'owns up' to all his petty illegalities? I remember a junior house-master addressing the assembled boys at length on the subject of Honour; the occasion was quite typical. A dirty and unmarked gym shoe had been left in the changing-room, and he called on the boy to 'own up'. The boy, being more adult than the master, naturally did nothing of the kind. But the Honour of the whole house was at stake and the whole house was punished, an implicit encouragement to us to discover and lynch the offender. I cannot see any moral distinction between a rope for a negro and a knotted towel for a boy.

More seriously harmful was the sexual standard. I doubt if there was a more appallingly innocent school in existence at that time. By innocent I mean that its humour was lavatory humour and not straightfor-wardly sexual. You will notice in Mr. Lyon's article the typical pedagogue's attitude to sexual humour, which he calls smut (I suppose the world may be divided into those who enjoy *Punch* and those who enjoy the *New Yorker*). Very rarely a boy was expelled. I can only remember one case. It is a curious system, but one common to all public schools, which prevents a normal sexual relationship and punishes harshly any temporary substitute. It is the method of the State which offers no other means than theft to an unemployed man to feed his family adequately and then punishes him when he steals. One notices in Miss Theodora Benson's article how much more sensibly her school treated the matter. A girl's 'rave' there did not, apparently, lead to an expulsion, not even to a heavy conversation with the house-mistress. (Lesbianism in this country has never been a criminal offence.) But Miss Arnot Robertson's devastating essay prevents any rash generalization in favour of girls' schools.

There is a curious distaste in this country for purely destructive criticism. It is as if no house-breakers could be employed who were not fellows of the R.I.B.A. What, it will be demanded, can one offer in place of the present system? The grammar school, which at one time gave perhaps the best education, seems to have lost its independence by aping the public school. In theory the co-educational school seems to me ideal, but Mr. Grant Watson's essay indicates that at one time co-education was just as sexually repressive as the old system. There is no advantage in educating girls and boys together if an unnaturally 'safe' tone is preserved by laughing at any sentimental relationship. A 'comradely' no-nonsense-about-sex attitude between men and women is peculiarly repellant. There is an air of unreality about the whole business of co-education in England, a combination of rather conscious daring and rather secret prudence.

Perhaps there is too much of the old Adam in me to welcome any more than Mr. Verschoyle does the progressive schools with their intensive sympathy for children and their blithe belief in the perfectibility of human nature. Already they seem a little out of date like a Bernard Shaw play. It is a penalty of progress; the public school, which has never progressed and never had contact with the serious thought of any age, remains for that reason ageless. It is a little pathetic that, at a period when socialists and conservatives alike are losing faith in Parliamentary government, the most advanced schools preserve the charming old-fashioned idealistic views of the early Fabians (even the sandals seem a relic of Walter Crane) and practise self-government of an extreme Parliamentary kind.

The example of Norway is a better one, I think, for us to follow. There State education has become almost universal during the last ten years, but State education robbed of its particular perils, a State education in the hands of non-political Civil Servants.

Education has become in England too broad a term and the child has lost the independence which was his in the days of the old village school, when he was taught certain subjects and prepared for certain exams and not 'educated for life', when his personality was not the prey of sex-ridden pedagogues or experimental psychologists or politicians. For the wider education can safely be left to the child and his natural curiosity. He will pick up all he needs to know in the fields or in the streets; because so much of his time is free, and his speculation endless, he will soon know as much as his elders who are confined to their desks. He may not grow up as a successful colonial administrator in the English tradition, but he will be an adult, which is more than can be said for most of the men we send abroad to rule.

He will have learnt sex more truthfully in a farm yard than in a house-master's study; and if he is a town child the jokes written on lavatory walls are likely to do less harm than the sentimentality, the embarrassment, the intellectual flummery of a set talk before confirmation on 'the facts of life'. They will have taught him at any rate that sexual enjoyment is neither solemn nor dull.

When he is released from work (I am still thinking of the State schools as enlargements of the old village school), his town and not his school will offer him the opportunity for sport. Games and school I should like to see kept rigidly apart, for games are used more than anything else to teach him narrow loyalties (that they do not teach him sportmanship is obvious in any football match between rival public schools). It is at least better that he should learn loyalty to a town which includes all classes and both sexes than to an institution consisting only of his own sex and his own class.

Why, in any case, he should feel more loyal to a school which is paid to teach him than to a butcher who is paid to feed him I cannot understand. I am afraid my want of understanding is responsible for this book.

MORE OXFORD PAPERBACKS

Details of other Oxford Paperbacks are given on the following pages. A complete list of Oxford Paperbacks including the World's Classics, Twentieth-Century Classics, Oxford Shakespeare, Oxford Authors, Past Masters, and OPUS series, can be obtained in the UK from the General Publicity Department, Oxford University Press, Walton Street, Oxford, OX2 6DP.

In the USA, complete lists are available from the Paperbacks Marketing Manager, Oxford University Press, 200 Madison Avenue, New York, NY 10016.

The Heirs of Tom Brown
The English School Story

Isabel Quigly

The Heirs of Tom Brown is an entertaining and original investigation into the literary, social, and cultural history of the school story in the heyday of the English Public School. Isabel Quigly discusses her chosen stories in relation to the themes which recur most frequently throughout the genre – the cult of games, the love story, the boarding school as a training ground for the Empire, schoolboy heroics, and an extraordinary preoccupation with death. Her selection ranges from such masterpieces as *Stalky & Co.* and Wodehouse's cricketing stories, to the schoolgirl tales of Angela Brazil, and the scandalously subversive *The Loom of Youth*.

'an excellent guide to this curious but interesting chapter in social and literary history' *Listener*

Some People

Harold Nicolson

New introduction by Nigel Nicolson

The story of author and diplomat Sir Harold Nicolson's relationship with his wife, Vita Sackville West, was described by their son Nigel in his celebrated book *Portrait of a Marriage*. Nigel Nicolson has now written an introduction to *Some People*, his father's highly original autobiography of his childhood, years at Oxford, and career in the Foreign Office. In nine brilliant vignettes Harold Nicolson puts 'real people in imaginary situations, and imaginary people in real situations' to create a careful self-portrait and an acute, sometimes mordant, commentary on people he had known, and on fashionable life in the 1920s.

'one of the most entertaining insights into the intellectual and social elite of the early twentieth century' *The Times*

First Childhood
and
Far from the Madding War

Lord Berners

Preface by Sir Harold Acton

This volume couples Lord Berners' childhood autobiography with one of his novels, as an introduction to this extraordinary author. Diplomat, composer, painter, as well as writer, Lord Berners grew up in a very proper Victorian household. In *First Childhood* he describes with characteristic wit and charm, his early experiences of family and school life. *Far from the Madding War* is a work of fiction, set in wartime Oxford, which mingles fantasy and satire.

'It is a bargain and a delight – particularly the autobiography . . . by any standards an absorbing book'
Times Literary Supplement

'Lord Berners spices his very funny account of a rather isolated and unhappy childhood . . . with a wicked wit'
British Book News

The Adventures of Mr Verdant Green

Cuthbert Bede

Introduction by Anthony Powell

As his name suggests, Mr Verdant Green is a gullible
innocent. When he leaves his country home to attend
Brazenface College, Oxford, he finds himself the butt
of practical jokes, swindles, and hoaxes played on him
by more worldly men. His career at the University is
the subject of this hilarious comedy, first published
between 1853 and 1857, and one of the earliest examples of the 'Oxford novel'. The book is profusely and
delightfully illustrated by the author, Edward Bradley,
whose pseudonym of Cuthbert Bede is an amalgam of
the names of the patron saints of his real *alma mater*,
Durham.

'Reading "The Adventures" is very much the same as
reading a guide book of a century ago about somewhere one knows today, a journey of discovery and
nostalgia mingled, and a delight into the bargain.'
Daily Telegraph.

P. G. Wodehouse
A Literary Biography

Benny Green

'A fine study not superseded by Frances Donaldson's recent authorized biography. Green's analysis of Orwell and Wodehouse, for example, is revelatory.' *Sunday Times*

'An affectionate and witty biography reminding us how dull the world would be without the antics of Wodehouse's amiable lunatics.' *Sunday Telegraph*